POLITICS, TECHNOLOGY, AND
BUREAUCRACY IN
SOUTH ASIA

INTERNATIONAL STUDIES
IN
SOCIOLOGY AND SOCIAL ANTHROPOLOGY

General Editor

K. ISHWARAN

VOLUME XXXVI

YOGENDRA MALIK (ED.)

POLITICS, TECHNOLOGY, AND
BUREAUCRACY IN
SOUTH ASIA

LEIDEN — E. J. BRILL — 1983

POLITICS, TECHNOLOGY, AND BUREAUCRACY IN SOUTH ASIA

EDITED BY

YOGENDRA K. MALIK

LEIDEN — E. J. BRILL — 1983

ISBN   90 04 07027 3

PRINTED IN THE NETHERLANDS BY E. J. BRILL

Politics, Technology, and Bureaucracies
An Overview

YOGENDRA K. MALIK

University of Akron, Akron, U.S.A.

SURINDER M. BHARDWAJ

Kent State University, Kent, U.S.A.

Technology, whether high, soft path, or appropriate, has become the buzzword in the Third World development literature. Whether the focus is on technology transfer, the broader issue of "North-South" dialogue, the diffusion processes within an emerging country, the horizontal or lateral technology flow within the "South" or the human consequences of technology, the word "technology" conjours up a varied and expectant imagery in the mind.

Since the start of the decolonization process, the societies in South Asia have been constantly engaged in achieving two interrelated goals: (a) political consolidation and nation building and, (b) modernization of their societies through the diffusion of technology and through economic growth. The process of political decolonization is over and inspite of the internal ethnic-cultural divisions existing within these societies, and the weak development of national identities, further disintegration of the state system existing in South Asia is not likely to take place in view of the "stabilization of the global military situation" (Suvant, 3: 1: 1981: 48-61). Modernization is, therefore, presently the most important goal before these societies. Along with the political questions related to the institutional structure existing within them, the strategies and policies in the area of modernization through technology transfer are, however, being questioned (Frankel, 1971: Franda: 1979).

In this essay we try to pull together some of the ideas of the contributors to this volume and set them in the broader context of technology transfer-appropriate technology theme. We then try to identify five major groups of decision-makers within the development/modernization literature and to indicate some implications of their mutual interaction for appropriate technology generation and transfer.

We begin with the simple notion that the fundamental bases of any cultural system are (a) the biophysical environment resources, (b) systems of ideas, beliefs, and values, (c) the nature of the institutional structure and organization, and (d) the nature and level of its technology. The ideological, institutional, and technological components of the culture are interlinked, so that significant change in any one is likely to have repercussions throughout the entire system. When any society sets upon the path of modernization, the modernization modes will influence the nature of production, the ecological consequences of the latter, and the social, cultural, and political processes and configurations. The different contributions in this volume may therefore be viewed within the framework below:

Interactions in a Cultural System

Focus of the Contributing Authors

Contributor	Main Argument	Result/Impact
Agnew	Theoretical screening	Identification of appropriate theoretical framework for *technology* transfer
Yapa	Advocacy of basic goods, biogenic diet and access to health care	Development and diffusion of *appropriate technology*
Malik	Degree of technological exposure	*Ideological change* (belief and value formulation)
Vajpeyi	Elite ideological commitment/choice	Nature of technological/ institutional preferences
Kennedy	Elite Conflict	*Institutional* Change/ Challenge
Somjee	Elite complementarity and cooperation	Development of an emulative model

"Ideology" in the preceding framework is assumed to include ideas, beliefs, values, principles, choices, theoretical orientations and commitments. Technology here implies the application of scientific principles toward solving specific problems. "Appropriate" technology by derivation, then, is the application of scientific principles toward solving problems within a particular cultural context. "Institutions" in our diagram implies all the structural and organizational arrangements (economic, social, political, governmental, legal, etc.) of the society.

Agnew argues that all theories of development, not just the "diffusionist" theories, need to be critically evaluated with respect to their implications in technology transfer. This argument helps to generalize the issue of technology transfer and appropriate technology and makes it a logical necessity to converge toward theories which clearly focus on the provision of basic human needs without adverse ecopolitical consequences.

Yapa develops and advocates specifically the theory that has at least three interlinked desirable and achievable results for the developing economies; the selection of an appropriate technology, which helps in achieving the provision of basic goods for the masses without adverse ecopolitical consequences. Crucial to the entire theory is the choice of and diffusion of appropriate technologies. Although development literature in general tends to identify the concept "appropriate technology" with technology for the developing countries, in fact many technologies, including some agricultural and industrial technologies, may have become inappropriate even for the industrialized countries. "Appropriate" should not be merely a euphemism reserved for the Third World technologies.

Dhirendra Vajpeyi explores the relationships between ideological choice of the Indian elites, i.e., commitment to egalitarianism and industrialization, and the increasing manifestation of democratic and secular motifs in the social and political institutions. He is optimistic about the ability of the Indian political elite, buttressed by their desirable belief structure, to propel India toward a modernized egalitarian nation.

Malik explores the relationship between technological exposure of the Indian youth and modernistic belief formulation among them. Thus, a higher degree of technological exposure is empirically found to be positively correlated with a moderate political orientation and a preference for a consumption-oriented economic system.

Kennedy examines the tension between two elite institutional segments in Pakistan—the "technocrats" and the "generalist" bureaucrats within the modernization paradigm, resulting in a challenge to the heretofore unquestioned superior hierarchical position of the "generalist". This is, in fact, part of the larger change in the value orientation, and consequent demands for institutional reorganization as modernization proceeds. In contrast Somjee demonstrates that in the absence of bureaucratic intervention and with the grant of autonomy to the technocrats and the cooperation of politicians the technocrats are able to build modern institutional/organizational network to achieve rationally and scientifically oriented goals.

The value premises of the elites empirically studied in this volume generally include a Western rationalistic orientation, preference for a consumption-oriented economy, egalitarian ideals, and a vision of modernity based on science and technology. The implications of these value premises on the issue of technology transfer and appropriate technology generation can be profound since the elites constitute the crucial components of the development policy evaluation, articulation, and implementation. However, in spite of the rhetoric of appropriate technology transfer, or its indigenous development, there is instead some impulsion toward a high energy consumption orientation among the rising middle and upper classes. The purchase of what has been known as "packaged technology" and "Turn Key industrial projects" from advanced and industrialized societies has become common (Zahlan, 1978: XI). A key issue, however, is whether or not such technology is indeed appropriate given the current conditions of widespread unemployment and income disparity.

The Issue of "Appropriate Technology"

The issue of "appropriate technology" has been popular ever since the seminal work of Amartya Kumar Sen—*Choice of Technique* (Sen, 1962). Almost a quarter of a century ago he argued, on the basis of comparison of certain cotton weaving techniques, Western and indigenous Indian, that the choice of a technique ultimately is not merely an engineering problem of efficiency but a human problem within a particular cultural context (Sen, 1962: 114). Whether a particular tool, technique, artifact, or production system will be "adopted" by a culture axiomatically entails choice. A fundamental question is, of course, related to the decision makers, the pace setters, the key 'agents' whose choices may determine whether or not an otherwise "appropriate" technology will diffuse and what consequence in the social, political, and environmental domains it will generate.

"Appropriate technology" by its very definition requires that we avoid making sweeping generalizations about it. Talking about the diffusion, transfer, or appropriateness of a given technology for the Third World Countries is meaningless unless the differences between and even within them are "appropriately" understood. At a conference of the International Economic Association, Robinson observed that "there are not two alternative appropriate technologies—one appropriate to advanced countries and one appropriate to less developped countries" (Robinson, 1979: 29). He went on to argue in favor of a "hierarchy of technologies appropriate to countries with a variety of scarcities and surplus of different factors" (Robinson, 1979: 29). Much earlier, Sen had stressed the need to avoid lumping together all the Less Developed Countries for some collectively 'appropriate' technology because the "degree of economic, social and cultural heterogeneity is considerably greater among countries which have not experienced the industrial revolution than among countries which have" (Sen, 1962: 12). In addition, the natural resource endowment differs substantially within the Third World Countries. What is "appropriate" for the vast, under populated, hot and wet Amazonia in Latin America may differ greatly from the sparsely populated water deficient Sahel or the Rajasthan Desert region. The agricultural technology is bound to be different in the densely populated water surplus Kerala as compared to the water deficient, unirrigated interior regions of India. Thus, the rhetoric of appropriate technology must be tempered by an understanding of the regional and even local cultural-institutional framework and the resource base. The same lesson is brought home by the experience of the "Green Revolution" (Pray, 1981: 68).

Critchfield, in a recent article points out that there are "six main cultural variations in the rural Third World: Confucian, Malay-Javanese, Hindu, Christian, Islamic and African" (Critchfield, 1982: 23). It is not necessary to agree with all his reasoning, projecting future development within the framework of cultural determinism, to appreciate the fundamental differences between the responses of these six cultures to the impact of modern technology and appropriate technology transfer. He argues fervently in favor of preserving the village cultures through a speedy diffusion of a most appropriate technology, e.g. rural electrification (Critchfield, 1982: 38).

In general, it is maintained in the appropriate technology literature that emphasis must be given to employment intensification. In other words, a technology transfer that threatens to generate unemployment by substituting capital for labor must be discouraged. Such a point of view is questioned by those who argue that appropriate technology which emphasizes high employment could also mean lower than minimum wages for the workers due to lowered productivity (Baron, 1980: 32-33). Baron believes that in "real economies, and in actual choices of technology, it is inevitably the financial revenues and costs which guide the decisions" (Baron, 1980: 33). A substantially different viewpoint is presented by others. Jequier, for example, is not impressed by the economic argument alone, and maintains that the appropriateness of a particular technology depends upon a number of social, cultural and technical factors which may be difficult to quantify but are no less important than the economic factors (Jequier, 1979: 2). Jequier also warns against the assumption that appropriate technology is a second-rate technology because designing even a truly efficient oxcart can be conceptually as challenging as industrial innovations (Jequier, 1979: 3). Moreover, the fact that a given technology is simple or simplified is no assurance of its appropriateness. Ultimately, the appropriatness must be determined within the cultural milieu, for appropriate technology "is not and should not be viewed as a second-best solution...appropriate and modern technologies are complementary rather than contradictory" (Jequier, 1979: 3). We should not assume either that only the Third World oriented technology should be culturally sensitive. Scholars are increasingly emphasizing the need to examine the environmental, social, and political context of modern technology in the more developed countries (Hannay and McGinn, 1980: 25-51).

"Technopolitics"

The issue of appropriate technology linked as it is with the views of the policymakers and the opinionmakers, cannot be divorced from politics. It has been suggested that artifacts do have politics, even though they may not have been designed with politics in mind (Winner, 1980: 121-136). Winner supports the view that certain technologies, such as dispersed solar, are more conducive to cultural pluralism, freedom and equity than the highly centralized energy systems such as natural gas and electric power (Winner, 1980: 121). Similarly, Critchfield observed "a sense of freedom" being experienced by the "Sikh untouchables" of Punjab who not too long ago "were forced to sit on the ground and use no utensils or water vessels in a landlord's house..." (Critchfield, 1982: 27). This social change is certainly part of the politics of untouchability, related to the Green Revolution technology's impact. Yapa in this volume has rightly observed that when innovations are biased in favor of a high dose of capital, they can scarcely be expected to favor the poor. In a similar vein, Winner cites a lawsuit filed by California Rural Legal Assistance against the University of California charging that the university officials spend tax money on projects that benefit a few private interests rather than the farmworkers (Winner, 1980: 126). Innovations focusing on mass transportation can be expected to be more egalitarian in their political impact in the developing countries than those emphasizing personal automobiles. Nevertheless, the Indian government has given permission to Maruti-Suzuki to produce personal automobiles.

Reddy, like Yapa, stresses the need for the generation of appropriate technology to specifically advance three main objectives: basic human needs, endogenous self-reliance, and harmony with the environment (Reddy, 1979: 173). The decision to focus on such technology is replete with politics, as he goes on to propose specific environmental, economic, and social "preferences". He proposes, for example, preference for technologies based upon renewable resources, that are more decentralized, thus creating employment opportunities for the masses rather than the elite, and that facilitate the flow of power to the people rather than concentrating it in the hands of the elite (Reddy, 1979: 178-179). He goes so far as to propose that the linkages between the Research and Development Institutions and the elites be drastically weakened so that technology suited to their desires and demands is discouraged (Reddy, 1979: 186-187).

Not the least important aspect of 'technopolitics' is the implication of appropriate technology for the women. A number of studies have recently drawn attention to this aspect (Dauber and Cain, 1981; D'Onofrio-Flores and Pfafflin, 1982). The variety of new roles, opportunities and challenges for the women in the Third World will be affected by the nature of technology and its diffusion.

When we examine India's Green Revolution technology from the political angle, two very different and contradictory political consequences can be pointed out. On the one hand there was a substantial increase in grain production (especially wheat) which made India, as a nation, more self-assured and politically less subject to coercion from the grain surplus countries. On the other hand, the internal impact has been very complex, accentuating the inter-

"multinational corporations, especially those involved in consumer industries, play a significant role in the diffusion of modern consumer culture to developing societies. They often succeed in creating needs for the commodities and services that are not desirable in view of the overall poverty of the LICS. They are, therefore, instruments in promoting glaring disparities in the consumption patterns of different segments of the population" (Kumar, 1979: 14). If the advertisements and the commercials appearing in the popular magazines, newspapers, and on the billboards displayed prominently in the urban centers of population are any guide, it is evident that, besides the multinationals, native monopoly business and industrial houses who operate in the protective markets are also engaged in promoting the values associated with culture based upon high consumption. Native industrial and business organizations "in their haste to service a newly-growing middle class market...have simply bought off-the-shelf technology from developed countries and concentrated on marketing and selling. They, for reasons of profit or otherwise, may have failed to invest in the research and development that would enable the products to remain current with world standards" (Stevens, *New York Times*, 1982: 17-18). In auto manufacturing, for instance, Indian industrialists have collaborated with their British and Italian counterparts, but unlike the Japanese who collaborated with the U. S. and developed their own technology, Indian industrialists have done little to improve upon the borrowed technology. If societies of South Asia, particularly India, "cannot develop their own home-grown technical innovations, it is reasoned that the gap between the 'Northern' and the 'Southern' hemispheres in science-based wealth and power will not only continue but will probably widen" (Stevens, *New York Times*, 1982: 18).

5. *Academic and Intellectual Establishments* within the societies of South Asia, especially in India, as well developed and have a well-defined role. Many of the institutions of modern learning were established by the British Government in India, and by the time the British left India these had developed into respectable centers for learning and for the advancement of modern knowledge. Since the independence of these countries, there have been enormous increases in the numbers of universities and colleges engaged in the pursuit and diffusion of scientific and technical knowledge. Over a period of time, many of these institutions have become highly bureaucratized or politicized. Not only is there a lack of innovative research and dynamism in academic circles, but a lack of integration of these institutions of higher learning into the ongoing process of technological and industrial revolution taking place within these societies. It is a matter of common knowledge that neither the government nor industry take advantage of the research and information originating within the universities. Although the Indian intellectual establishment, outside academic circles, has challenged the strategies related to the transfer and diffusion of technology adopted by the elites—the bureaucrats, administrators, and politicans have paid very little attention to social science research. Social scientists such as economists, cultural anthropologists, and sociologists, etc. can help in the adaptation of modern technology to the cultural and environmental concerns

of any society. In India the government and the various government sponsored institutions are the largest employers of social scientists. The government has also established policy-oriented research institutions which have been able to undertake research on policy related issues. However, such research has little impact on actual policy formulation. Referring to the Indian situation, Professor M. Weiner observes that, "administrators do not pay much attention to the social science research, they term it 'too academic, too removed from social reality', while social scientists find the government system 'is so vast, so complex, so immobile' that any kind of change and innovation are difficult" (Weiner, 1979: 1622). Very rarely do the members of the academic community or the social scientists from the research institutions hold office or advise on crucial policy issues. Even though members of the academic community and Indian intellectual establishment unlike the western societies, help in the diffusion of innovative ideas and concepts, there is no development of partnership between the universities and research institutions, on the one side, and the government and the industry on the other.

Thus, the five 'elites' briefly described above do not seem to form a well-integrated culture for appropriate technology development and technological transfer. Being partly at cross purposes, and partly self-centered, their actions frequently do not mesh to create a clear development direction. Efforts related to the transfer of technology will be more fruitful if the interactions of these elites are more clearly understood. Certainly, it will be in the national interest of India to articulate technology policies which the various elite components have developed in harmony.

Conclusions

Recognizing the limits of both space and of the scope of this discussion, we have made a modest effort to identify the socio-cultural background of the actors involved in making technological choices. Under the conditions we can only draw attention to certain important implications which will be further verified by future research. There seems to have developed a kind of ruling structure within societies in South Asia. This structure consists of politico-bureaucratic and industrial elites. These are more or less able to determine the goals and the direction of transfer and diffusion of technology. The initial goals of technology transfer, namely, to increase economic productivity, to satisfy the basic needs for essential goods and services—enough food, adequate shelter, public transportation, health and educational facilities—are still far from realization. In 1977-78 it was estimated that in India alone around 48 percent of the population in rural areas and 41 percent in urban areas still lived below the proverty level. The total number of such people living in abject poverty comes close to 300 million. As of recent times, observations on the government's spendings in technology and production related policies show that "an unduly large share of resources is...absorbed in production which related directly or indirectly to maintaining or improving the living standards of higher income groups (*E.P.W.*, 1979: 1220).

Intra-elite rivalry, furthermore, limits the full utilization of the national potential and capabilities for technological self-reliance. An awareness of the class nature of the imported technology and the class-biased decisions in terms of technology transfer is growing. Independent intellectuals realize the ''need for alternate technology'' based upon rigorous scientific research suited to the indigenous environment and leading to self-reliance (Kumar and Reddy, 1977). Alternate technology does not, of course, mean watered-down technology.

There is also a growing awareness about the danger of the gradual over-taking of the native thinking and value system by what has been termed ''cultural imperialism'' (Galtung, 8, 1971: 81-117). Even if one does not completely accept all the implications of the concept of cultural imperialism, it can hardly be denied that acceptance of the values associated with high consumption-oriented cultures of advanced industrial societies has already significantly affected the behavior patterns of the ruling elites in South Asia.

If the elites continue to propagate the value orientation that they now have, they may be forced to both accept and resent national dependence on the West. Furthermore, the social economic and political distance between the urban centers and the rural masses will only increase, not to mention the inter-regional imbalance already in existence. The political cost of such spatial economies could be considerable. How to achieve a degree of disengagement from such a situation? How to maintain a degree of cultural autonomy? These are difficult questions. In an open and relatively free society, like India, it becomes all the more difficult to decide how to achieve a balance between fair distribution and technological development, between selective borrowing from the west and the preservation of the essentials of the native culture, between Gandhian principles of rural-oriented technological innovations consequent on economic growth, and defense-oriented technological self-reliance? There do not seem to be any easy answers. However, the continuous and conspicuous consumption by the elite segment of society and the political and electoral mobilization of the disadvantaged sectors of the Indian population, may not co-exist in peace and stability for an indefinite period of time.

REFERENCES

Ahmad, Aqueil
    1978   ''Science and Technology in Development: Policy Options for India and China'', *Economic and Political Weekly*, December. pp. 2074-2090.
Balasubramanyam, V. N.
    1973   *International Transfer of Technology to India*. New York, Praeger.
Baron, C.
    1980   ''Technological Choice and Transfer in Food Processing in Developing Countries: An Overview'', in Christopher G. Baron (ed.), *Technology, Employment and Basic Needs in Food Processing in Developing Countries*. Oxford, Pergamon.

BHATT, V. V.
    1981 "Development Problem, Strategy and Technology Choice: Sarvodaya and
          Socialistic Approaches in India", *Economic Development and Cultural Change*, Vol. 31,
          No. 1, pp. 85-99.
BROOKS, Harvey
    1980 "Technology, Evolution and Purpose", *Daedalus*, Vol. 109, No. 1, Winter,
          pp. 65-81.
CAIN, Melinda L.
    1981 "Overview: Women and Technology—Resources for our Future" in Roslyn
          Dauber and Melinda L. Cain (eds.) *Women and Technological Change in Developing
          Countries*. Boulder, Westview Press.
CRITCHFIELD, Richard
    1982 "Science and the Villager: The Last Sleeper Wakes", *Foreign Affairs*, Vol. 61, No. 1,
          Fall, pp. 14-41.
DAUBER, Roslyn and Melinda L. CAIN (eds.)
    1981 *Women and Technological Change in Developing Countries*. Boulder, Colorado, Westview
          Press.
DESAI, Ashok
    1979 "U. S. Corporations as Investors in India: A Study of their Experiences,
          1955-1978", *Economic and Political Weekly*, pp. 2015-2021.
D'ONOFRIO-FLORES, Pamela M. and Sheila M. PFAFFLIN (eds.)
    1982 *Scientific-Technological Change and the Role of Women in Development*. Boulder, Colorado,
          Westview Press.
Economic and Political Weekly
    1978 December, p. 1220.
Economic and Political Weekly
    1979 August.
The Economist,
    1983 "The Day of the Scorpion", *The Economist*, January 8, 1983, pp. 64-67.
ENCARNATION, Dennis J.
    1979 "The Indian Central Bureaucracy: Responsive to Whom?" *Asian Survey*,
          November, pp. 1126-1145.
EVENSON, Robert E.
    1981 "Benefits and Obstacles to Appropriate Agricultural Technology", *Annals* AAPSS,
          Vol. 458, November, pp. 54-67.
FRANKEL, Francine
    1978 *India's Political Economy, 1947-1977*. Princeton, N. J., Princeton University Press.
FRANDA, Mark
    1979 *India's Rural Development: An Assesssment of Alternatives*. Bloomington, Indiana Univer-
          sity Press.
GALTUNG, John
    1971 "Structural Theory of Imperialism", *Journal of Peace Research*, Vol. 8, August,
          pp. 81-117.
HANNAY, N. Bruce and Robert E. McGINN
    1980 "The Anatomy of Modern Technology: Prolegomenon to an Improved Public
          Policy for the Social Management of Technology", *Daedalus*, Vol. 109, No. 1,
          Winter, pp. 25-54.
JEQUIER, N.
    1979 "Technology: Some Criteria" in A. S. Bhalla (ed.) *Towards Global Action for Ap-
          propriate Technology*. Oxford, Pergamon Press.
KUMAR, Amalya and N. REDDY *et al.*
    1977 *Problems in the Generation and Diffusion of Appropriate Technologies*. (memeographed)
          Bangalore, Indian Institute of Science.
KUMAR, Krishna (ed.)
    1979 *Bonds Without Bondage: Explorations in Transcultural Interactions*. Honolulu, East-West
          Center, The University of Hawaii.

KUMAR, Krishna (ed.)
  1980 *Transnational Enterprises: Their impact on Third World Societies and Cultures*. Boulder, Colorado, Westview Press.
LANDE, Carl H.
  1976 "Technocrats in Southeast Asia: A Symposium", *Asian Survey*, December, pp. 1151-1155.
NEHRU, Jawaharlal
  1946 *Discovery of India*. New York, Doubleday.
PRAY, Carl E.
  1981 "The Green Revolution as a Case Study in Transfer of Technology", *Annals* AAPSS, Vol. 458, November, pp. 68-80.
REDDY, Amulya Kumar
  1979 "Problems in the Generation of Appropriate Technologies" in Austin Robinson (ed.) *Appropriate Technologies for Third World Development*. New York, St. Martin's Press, pp. 173-189.
ROSENTHAL, Donald
  1970 "Deurbanization, Elite Displacement and Political Change in India", *Comparative Politics*, Vol. 14, No. 2. pp. 169-201.
ROBINSON, Austin
  1979 "The Availability of Appropriate Technologies", in Austin Robinson (ed.) *Appropriate Technologies for Third World Development*. New York, St. Martin's Press, pp. 26-44.
SAMBRANI, Shreekant and Palin K. GARG
  1979 "Brave New World of Young Indian Decision Making Elite", *Economic and Political Weekly*, August, pp. 14-95-100.
SEN, Amartya Kumar
  1962 *Choice of Techniques*. Oxford, Basil Blackwell.
SHARMA, Ram D. R.
  1979 "Selection of Civil Services", *Economic and Political Weekly*, January, p. 141.
STEVENS, William K.
  1982 "India: Once a Giant in Science: Tries to Rekindle the Creative Fire", *New York Times*, November 9, pp. 18-19.
SUVANT, Karl
  1981 "From Economic to Socio-Cultural Emancipation: The Historical Context of the New International Economic Order and in New International Socio-Cultural Order", *Third World Quarterly*, Vol. 3, No. 1, pp. 48-61.
WEINER, M.
  1979 "Social Science Research and Public Policy in India", *Economic and Political Weekly*, September, pp. 1579-874 1622-28.
WINNER, Langdon
  1980 "Do Artifacts have Politics", *Daedalus*, Vol. 109, No. 1, Winter, pp. 121-136.
ZAHLAN, A. B.
  1978 *Technology Transfer and Change in the Arab World*. Oxford, Pergamon Press.

Technology Transfer and Theories of Development
Conceptual Issues in the
*South Asian Context**

JOHN A. AGNEW

Maxwell School, Syracuse University, Syracuse, U.S.A.

SOCIAL SCIENTISTS have often argued that technological change is a major source of economic growth and social change. Since new technologies are usually associated with a history of prior technological innovation, an important feature of technological change has been the diffusion of new technology from places of origin to users elsewhere. When such diffusion involves movement between two countries it is sometimes referred to as technology transfer. Technology in this context indicates knowledge of techniques of organization as well as technological innovations in the sense of machines, products and equipment.

The study of technology transfer as a division of the study of innovation diffusion is not well developed as an *explicit* focus of academic interest. Shannon R. Brown, for example, has written that:

> ...historical studies of technological change which are guided by an explicit theoretical framework are not yet very common, and among them, those which concentrate on the international transfer of technology are rarer still. Most of the studies of international transfer concentrate on transfers between similar countries, usually Great Britain and the United States (Brown 1979:550).

However, it is a basic premise of this paper that all theories of economic development and social change contain within them more or less *implicit* positions on the role and impact of technology transfer on development. Given some recent writing on the diffusion of innovations, this may seem a surprising claim (Blaikie, 1978; Browett, 1980). This literature has tended to single out a "bundle" of theories of development, variously described as modernization

* An earlier version of this paper was presented at the Tenth Annual Conference on South Asia, University of Wisconsin, Madison, Wisconzin, November 6-8, 1981. I would like to thank Priti Ramamurthy, Syracuse University, Dennis Conway, Indiana University, and Vijayan Pillai, University of Iowa for their helpful suggestions.

and neo-classical economic theories, and to label them as "diffusionist". The implication is that these theories emphasize diffusion (and technology transfer) while other theories do not. Hence, to study diffusion is to subscribe to a "diffusionist" theory. What is largely missing from the discussion but what may be the point of the argument is the assumption of the "diffusionist" theories of development that new technology is *invariably good* for those people and "countries" adopting it, i.e. that new technology leads directly to development and *worthwhile* social change. This, of course, is quite different from the impression this literature leaves that only those theories that *explicitly* discuss diffusion have a position on diffusion or technology transfer.

This paper is concerned with exploring the links between theories of development and positions on technology transfer. The set of development theories quoted is derived from an extensive reading in the literature but probably is not exhaustive. In addition, the distinctions drawn between some theories are open to dispute. The positions on technology transfer are based on a typology of diffusion perspectives that serves as an organizing principle in a recent book by Brown (1981). Research from a variety of contexts, especially South Asia, is used to suggest some major lacunae in *all* positions on technology transfer, whatever the development theory. This suggests that if one is interested in technology transfer, *all* development theories, not just those the critics have labelled "diffusionist", are in need of critical examination. Finally, the papers in this issue are discussed in terms of the contribution they make to resolving the problems of development theories with respect to technology transfer.

Theories of Development

A theory of development typically involves defining the concept "development" and providing a rationale for spatio-temporal differences in its extent. In most theories, "levels" of development equate with levels of economic growth. The definition of Havens and Flinn (1975:469) is fairly typical though more specific than most:

> Development...involves three interrelated societal activities: (1) the establishment of increased wealth and income as a perceived, attainable goal for the broader masses of [a] society; (2) the creation and/or selection of adequate means to attain this goal; and (3) the restructuring of society so that there is persistent economic growth.

There have been more or less sophisticated theories of development based upon such a definition for many years. But discussion of the term "development", indeed expropriation of the term for use in this context, is a relatively recent affair. Over the past twenty years "development studies" has come to constitute an increasingly large and vocal interdisciplinary field in social science. Within this field and associated areas of study, such as political development and cultural change, a range of theories has developed, drawing inspiration from a variety of intellectual traditions.

Three groups of theories can be identified in terms of the scale of analysis at which the theories operate and whether or not development is defined within them entirely in terms of the benefits of economic growth. The first group can be called "Modernization Theories". They focus on national societies as the basic units of analysis and define development in terms of economic growth and "Westernization", replicating the historical experience of Western societies (Tipps, 1973; Pletsch, 1981). The second group consists of theories that focus on the structure of economic and political relationships between "dominant" and "dominated" societies in the context of the global history of economic growth and political control (Evans, 1979; Agnew, 1982). They can be called "World Political Economy Theories". A third group takes an approach that involves a critical perspective on the purported benefits of development as usually defined and emphasizes the ecological and social/cultural disruption consequent to economic growth (Yapa, 1980). Currently this is the least known theory of development and involves the greatest departure from conventional wisdom.

Each of these groups of theories is actually and potentially divided by differences of emphasis, specificity and academic disciplinarianism. Table 1 contains a list of the theories. In some cases the identified "theory" covers a set of similar if not identical theories. This is the case, for example, with dual economy and modernity and institutional reform theories. This variety cannot be treated here and is not critical for the matter at hand.

Table 1

Theories of Development

Modernization	Stages of Growth
	Dual Economy
	Modernity
	Institutional Reform
	"Classic" Marxist
World Political Economy	Leninist
	Development of Underdevelopment
	World-System
	Multinational Corporation
Ecopolitical Economy	

The best known stages-of-growth theory is that of Rostow (1956, 1960). However, growth-stage theories have been a persistent feature of writing on development since the mid-nineteenth century (Hoselitz, 1969). Rostow identified in European economic history five stages of growth that can be used as a framework for national development whatever the particular context. Agriculture is a leading sector in the transition from "traditional" to "modern society". Technology plays an important role in development by transforming agriculture into a base for industrial growth. Commercialization of agriculture

Two general points are worth noting. First, the modernization theories tend to have a more positive view of technology transfer than do the other theories. This, of course, is the point noted, if not articulated clearly, by the critics of "diffusionism". Creating mechanisms for the supply of technology, developing infrastructure and/or improving the spread of knowledge about technology are thought to help development. Technological change through transfer facilitates economic growth. Second, none of the theories of development contains reference to the economic history perspective on technology transfer. Yet it is the economic history perspective that has generated the most empirical research on technology transfer and pinpointed the specific barriers to the easy transfer of technology from one setting to another (e.g. Rosenberg, 1970; Hayami, 1974; Saxonhouse 1974).

One important difference within the group of modernization theories is the difference between the modernity/institutional reform theories and the others. There has been a tendency to cluster modernization theories together in discussions of innovation diffusion but it is apparent that when regarded this way there are substantial differences between them. Specifically, the modernity and institutional reform theories focus on value change and Westernization as instruments for development. Thus, technology transfer will depend on receptiveness to innovation i.e. innovativeness. This corresponds most closely to the adoption perspective on technology transfer. The combination of a modernity theory of development and an adoption perspective on technology transfer is illustrated in a South Asian context by the work of Montagno (1978) and Morriss (1979). Somjee and Somjee (1978) provide an example of an institutional reform theory of development and an adoption perspective on technology transfer.

The other modernization theories, however, though they rest on assumptions concerning value orientations, are directed much more to the benefits that flow from the *supply* of technology and infrastructure. Technologies can be imposed *whatever* the initial outlook of "the natives". Economic and political barriers, not social or cultural ones, stand in the way of national development. Coercion or "marketing", in the promotional and advertising sense of the term, is the major mechanism for transformation. In the South Asia context the combination of a stages of growth theory of development and a market/infrastructure perspective on technology transfer is at the heart of work by Singh (1979), Ahluwalia (1978) and Mukherjee (1980). The classic Marxist tradition is also well-represented in this regional setting and also focuses on the supply of technology. Examples include Ghose (1979), Chattopadhay (1973), McAlpin (1975), and Saith (1981).

The other theories incorporate a more negative appraisal of technology transfer. Indeed, without exception that subscribe to the "development" perspective on technology transfer. Technology transfer is seen as beneficial to suppliers rather than adopters. It is also seen as "dependency creating". The technology in question is often *controlled* from elsewhere, may have negative effects in areas where it is introduced and may profit only those who sponsored its introduction (Weinstein and Pillai, 1979). Technology transfer also disrupts established and perhaps satisfactory social and ecological patterns. This literature is itself not well-developed in the South Asian context. There are only a few isolated works that combine a world political economy theory of development with a development perspective on technology transfer. Guha (1968) and Djurfeldt and Lindberg (1975) offer Leninist and "development of underdevelopment" theories of development, respectively, that have generally negative appraisals of technology transfer. Yapa (1980) provides an ecopolitical economy theory of development which has as one of its major components a development perspective on technology transfer.

All types of theories of development, therefore, contain positions on technology transfer. But it appears that these positions are partial and incomplete. For example, modernization theories have no place for *evaluating* the consequences of technology transfer. But world political economy theories also have deficiencies. In particular, they are usually silent on why patterns of control over technologies and other resources must *necessarily* lead to negative effects upon those to whom technologies are transferred. Technology transfer is *assumed* to be negative in its effects without examining the specific situations in which this might or might not be so.

Improving the Conceptualization of Technology Transfer in Theories of Development

How can theories of development be improved to account for the various aspects of technology transfer dealt with by the four perspectives on transfer? A first requirement is a clearer articulation of the relationship between development and technological change. An obvious strength of the world political economy theories is the critical *political* interpretation of technology transfer that they offer. Technology is viewed not just as technique but as contained within a web of constraining political relationships. Ecopolitical economy theory goes beyond this point to note, as well, the general ecological and cultural consequences of technological change. This theory opens to question whether "bigger is better" and whether capital-intensive is always superior to labor-intensive agriculture (e.g. on Sri Lanka and India, Yapa 1980). These are the hidden assumptions of modernization theories.

A second requirement is an examination of the political and economic conditions under which technology transfer has in the past led to economic growth. This is where the economic history perspective comes in. Economic historians interested in technology transfer have been concerned to identify the critical conditions under which technology transfer can be succesful. They focus on both local demand and local circumstances rather than engage in global generalizations. Hayami (1974) for example is concerned with the conditions for the diffusion of agricultural technology in Asia. He provides empirical evidence to suggest that in the Japanese case *local control* over decisions concerning technology transfer was vital:

The public sector played a critical role in [the] process of the development and diffusion of seed-fertilizer technology. Shortly after the Meiji Restoration, the government tried to modernize Japanese agriculture toward the large-scale mechanized farming of the Anglo-American type by importing Western farm machinery, crops, and livestock, and by inviting instructors from Britain and the United States. This policy of direct "technology borrowing" proved unsuccessful because of differences in both climatic and economic conditions. During the 1880's, the government quickly shifted to a strategy of agricultural development with the emphasis on raising yields of traditional food staples, above all, rice (Hayami 1974:139).

The importance of local *scope* for adopting or rejecting technology given local circumstances is emphasized by other economic historians (Evenson, 1974; Rosenberg, 1972; S. Brown, 1981; Weinstein and Pillai, 1979). Rosenberg (1972:33), a leading advocate of this viewpoint, summarizes as follows: "the productivity of any technology is never independent of its institutional context and therefore needs to be studied in that context". Unfortunately, theories of development have not incorporated this insight.

A third requirement involves the relative centrality of technology within theories of development. Many theories have regarded technology as secondary or even exogenous to the process of development. This is particularly true of economists and their modernization theories (Stewart, 1977). But this ignores the fact that "The technology available determines the boundaries of what it is possible for a country to do" (Stewart, 1977:xi). Improving the treatment of technology by incorporating notions of technical *choice* and *appropriate* technology is a necessary pre-requisite for improving the position of technology transfer in theories of development.

A fourth requirement concerns the ideology of the "technological imperative" and how it lays the groundwork for accepting a "marketing" message and, ultimately, acquiring a new technology. Authors such as Stanley (1978) and Mukerji (1983) point to the cultural underpinnings of what Stanley calls the "technological conscience" and Mukerji "the Western obsession with economic development and material comforts". Each is concerned, though in different ways, to explore the historical circumstances under which technical knowledge, a "more-is-better" ideology, and consumerism displace other value-orientations. Perhaps the adoption perspective can be reworked to examine these issues.

In particular, a question arises concerning the conditions under which a specific definition of development becomes widely accepted and associated with a particular set of technologies only available elsewhere. A recent paper by Bailes (1981) examines this question in the context of American technology transfer to the Soviet Union in the period 1917-1941. American technology and American methods of industrial production were much admired by the Bolshevik leaders and ironically, in view of later Soviet-American relations, the United States was in some respects a "model" for Soviet development (also Rogger, 1981). In particular, "the organization of American industry in large units of production, the application of techniques of mass production and standardization—the methods of Ford and Taylor in particular—were given much credit by Soviet writers for America's high level of labor productivity and rapid rate of growth in both industrial and agricultural production'' (Bailes, 1981:430).

A fifth requirement concerns the interaction between the growth of a Western-style mass education system and the type and rate of technology transfer. This relates to the previous point on the ideology of "developmentalism" but is a more specific aspect of it. Easterlin (1981) has argued that the "personal" element in technology transfer—demonstration, training, personal contact—presupposes a common intellectual and knowledge base and a common educational process. Some economic historians have been impressed by the significance of the "personal" element in technology transfer (Rosenberg, 1970; Cooper and Sercovich, 1970). For Easterlin, therefore:

> The educational system is...a key link between modern economic growth on the one hand, and a society's culture, on the other; study of the evolution of mass education provides an important clue as to when the net balance of the principal cultural forces in a society shifts in a direction favorable to economic growth (Easterlin 1981:14).

Of course, this presupposes the unimportance of economic and political barriers to growth other than the educational system, ignores the question of who benefits from growth and fails to address the question of whether growth is always synonymous with development. It is, nevertheless, an important point.

In sum, there are several specific respects in which all theories of development are deficient with regard to their conceptualizing of technology transfer. This, of course, is in addition to their collective failure to treat the technology transfer process in terms of all four perspectives on technology transfer. Some theories seem to be better able to incorporate *all* these aspects of technology transfer than others. Though open to a variety of criticisms, the world political economy theories and the ecopolitical economy theory provide a good base through their focus on the global setting of technology transfer and their historical orientation towards understanding development (Tomlinson, 1978; Evans, 1979; Agnew, 1982).

The Papers

The papers in this issue make a contribution towards improving the conceptualization of technology transfer within the bounds of two theories of development—modernity theory (Vajpeyi, Malik, Kennedy) and ecopolitical economy theory (Yapa)—and in the South Asian context. All are critical of technological determinism as an explanation of social change and all place technology transfer in an international setting. But here the similarities between the papers as a set, end. Vajpeyi, Malik and Kennedy emphasize the significance of value-orientations for technology transfer. Yapa stresses the nature of technology and the political-economic conditions under which it is supplied.

In terms of the specific ways of improving the conceptualizing of technology transfer in theories of development outlined above, Vajpeyi, Malik,

SOMJEE, A. H. and Geeta SOMJEE
1978 "Co-operative Dairying and the Profiles of Social Change in India", *Economic Development and Cultural Change*, Vol. 26, No. 3.
STANLEY, Manfred
1978 *The Technological Conscience: Survival and Dignity in an Age of Expertise*. New York: Free Press.
STEWART, Frances
1977 *Technology and Underdevelopment*. Boulder: Westview Press.
SWEEZY, Paul
1942 *The Theory of Capitalist Development*. London: Dobson.
TIPPS, Dean
1973 "Modernization Theory and the Comparative Study of Societies: A Critical Perspective", *Comparative Studies in Society and History*, Vol. 15, No. 2, pp. 199-226.
TOMLINSON, B. R.
1978 "Foreign Private Investment in India, 1920-1950", *Modern Asian Studies*, Vol. 12, No. 4, pp. 655-677.
WALLERSTEIN, Immanuel
1974 *The Modern World-System: Capitalist Agriculture and the Origins of the European World-Economy in the Sixteenth Century*. New York: Academic Press.
WALLMAN, Sandra (ed.)
1977 *Perceptions of Development*. Cambridge, England: Cambridge University Press.
WARREN, Bill
1980 *Imperialism: Pioneer of Capitalism*. London: New Left Books.
WEBER, Max
1958 *The Religion of India: The Sociology of Hinduism and Buddhism*. Glencoe, III.: Free Press.
WEINSTEIN, Jay and Vijayan K. PILLAI
1979 "Appropriate Technology versus Appropriating Technology: Alternative Approaches to the Transfer of Technology", Manuscript, Department of Social Science, Georgia Institute of Technology.
WESTERGAARD, K., H. SCHAUMBERG-MÜLLER, and K. NYHOLM
1976 "Livestock Adoption and Small Farmers" in S. D. Pillai (ed.), *Aspects of Changing India*, Bombay: Popular Prakashan.
WHARTON, Clifton R.
1963 "Research on Agricultural Development in Southeast Asia", *Journal of Farm Economics*, Vol. 45, pp. 1161-1174.
YAPA, Lakshman S.
1980 "Diffusion, Development and Ecopolitical Economy", in *Innovation Research and Public Policy*, edited by John A. Agnew, Syracuse: Syracuse University Geographical Series, No. 5.

Innovation Bias, Appropriate Technology, and Basic Goods

LAKSHMAN S. YAPA

The Pennsylvania State University, University Park, U.S.A.

MANY ECONOMISTS now concede that the goals of economic development in the third world can only be met through a direct attack on mass poverty by producing for basic needs first [13,25,29]. This has raised as a key issue the question of what technology to choose in the production of basic goods. "Intermediate", "alternative", "soft", or "appropriate", technology, as it is variously called, has a central role to play in the basic needs strategy of development because such technology is modest in it demand for capital, create many jobs, and use locally available resources [5,20,23]. Apart from these attributes of the actual "production forces" of appropriate technology, there are important "social" and "ecological relations" that need close examination. In previous work I have used the term "ecopolitical economy" to describe the holistic approach to the study of production forces taken together with both social and ecological relations of production [32,33]. Whoever controls the means of production and the development of innovations will determine what is produced, in what manner, and how the final income is distributed. These are called social relations of production and innovation. People engaging in production define relations not only among themselves, but also between production forces and nature. The latter are called ecological relations of production. Thus, the character of entrepreneurial innovation and economic production is determined in the larger matrix of ecopolitical economy: production + people + nature (Fig. 1).

Appropriate technology may be defined as those technologies that are best able to match the needs of all people in a society in a sustainable relationship with the environment [12: p. 187]. There are several important reasons why appropriate technology is essential to the success of the basic needs development strategy. First, the allocation of resources for basic needs will require a major political effort and appropriate technology has an important role to play in the organization and maintenance of that work. Second, the research and development of technology are basic mechanisms used in the reproduction of social relations of production. Certain types of technologies are developed and

encouraged because they are compatible with the dominant relations of production. Hence, programs for social change must necessarily take account of
the social implications of innovations. Third, mass production of basic goods
becomes possible only through the use of appropriate technology because these
technologies require far less capital than conventional ones. Finally, the
universal provision of basic goods must be ecologically sustainable in the long
run and this is possible only through the use of environmentally appropriate
technology. In this paper I shall explore some social and ecological relations of
production as they apply to economic development and the production of basic
goods. To do so I shall employ a concept which will be called the "K-biased innovation".

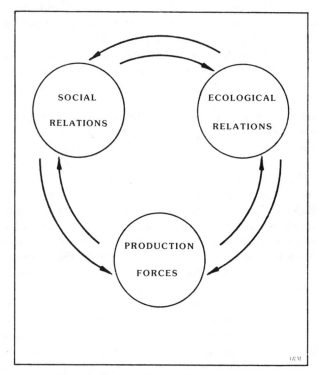

Fig. 1 A System of Ecopolitical Economy

Basic Goods and Opportunity Cost

For the purpose of this discussion I shall define basic goods as including
the following: a biogenic diet (that is, a diet which is adequate for growth and
maintenance of the human body), clothing, shelter, health care, and functional
literacy. Health care includes family planning, community hygiene, and
disease prevention.

The employment of a productive resource in one use implies the
unavailability of that resource for an alternative use. This is what economists

refer to as opportunity cost. For example, in India the production and use of private automobiles have an opportunity cost in such basic goods as bicycles and public transport which are foregone.

Using the U.S. definition of the poverty line, Nathan Keyfitz estimated that a "middle class" style of life consumed five times as much resources as the life of a poor person living below the poverty line. In 1975, there were four billion people in the world of whom 600 million enjoyed "middle class" styles of living. When the impact of middle-class consumption was taken into account it was as though the planet had not 4, but 6.4 billion to support [14]. The entry of people into the affluent middle class has a disproportionate effect on materials and environment compared with the increase in the number demanding basic goods. Following Keyfitz's line of reasoning and the concept of opportunity cost, it is possible to argue that in the third world the absence of basic goods at one level of society is causatively linked to the resouirce consumption of non-basic goods at another level of society. The prevalence of poverty and the absence of basic goods are a reflection of social choices made by society in the use of its resources. Poverty is the mirror image of the use of wealth by those who control it.

Development planners admit that a drastic restructuring of political and economic power is necessary if resources are to be directed to the production of basic goods for the masses. Such a struggle is primarily political. Marxian economists have consistently insisted on the primacy of the political element in economic development. This is evident from the basic Marxian premise that the development of production forces and the distribution of income are determined by social relation of production. Numerous writers working outside a Marxian mode of analysis including several religious workers have arrived at essentially the same conclusion, namely, that unequal access to resources is the primary factor in the persistence of mass poverty in the third world [16].

There can be no question that the production of basic goods will require major realignments in economic and political power. I shall not belabor this point because it is already well stated in the literature [1,18,22]. My aim in this paper is to examine the opposite relations, that is, the impact of production forces and the choice of technology on social and ecological relations of production. I shall argue here that the nature of production forces, particularly the choice of technology, will largely determine not only our ability to inaugurate a program for the production of basic goods but also to maintain such an economy in the long run. More specifically, I shall argue that the literature on appropriate technology, soft energy paths, organic agriculture, and so on is central to a development strategy based on providing for basic human needs first.

The Concept of K-biased Innovation

The impact of production forces on social and ecological relations of production will be examined through a concept which will be called the "K-biased

particularly oil and natural gas. U.S. agriculture is energy-intensive because of mechanization, irrigation, use of inorganic fertilizer and pesticides, and long distance transport of inputs and produce. The food system as a whole uses 10 kilocalories of energy for every single kilocalorie of food energy put on a table. If systems of food production worldwide adopted the energy standards of U.S. agriculture, over 80% of the world's fuel consumption would be required simply to feed the four billion people of today [24].

Extended use of nitrogen fertilizer affects soil structure adversely, and it reduces the capacity of the soil to obtain nitrogen naturally. This means that the more a farmer uses chemical nitrogen, the more he needs to maintain the productivity of the soil. Degradation of soil structure also accelerates soil erosion. In the U.S., three-fourths of the soil lost to running water is of agricultural origin. Furthermore the run-off from heavily fertilized fields causes the eutrophication of lakes and contaminates ground water [3].

When crops are selected for specific factors such as high yields, other features such as resistance to diseases are overlooked. With the increased vulnerability of crops, newer and more powerful pesticides are introduced. Continued use of powerful pesticides produces pests that develop pesticide resistance which results in the need for larger and larger doses. Most pesticides also kill non-target populations, thus freeing formerly harmless pests from their natural controls. Pesticides which do not degrade in nature pass along the food chain and pose a direct threat to human and animal health. Thus, increased use of chemical fertilizer and pesticides has trapped the American farmer in a vicious cycle. Crop loss through soil degradation, erosion, and resistant pests compels the farmer to use more fertilizer and pesticides, and the spiral builds to a climax of contaminated water, exhausted soil, higher costs, and lower profits [19].

Monoculture is a basic fact of modern agriculture. Indeed the story of agriculture is one of declining plant variety and this loss of genetic variety has been accelerated by the development of high-yielding varieties. Ninety-five percent of food comes from no more than 30 plants. Simply planting extensive monocultures invites diseases. In 1970 about 17% of the U.S. corn crop was lost to a corn-leaf blight and about 80% of the crop was susceptible to this disease. Most major crops in the U.S. are genetically very uniform and hence vulnerable to disease. According to plant geneticists, the most serious consequence of Green Revolution agriculture is the accelerating loss of genetic variety [9].

Productive as it is, U.S. farming follows a hard path which is not sustainable in the long-run. Therefore, we have to question the conventional wisdom of increasing food production through the diffusion of hard path farming technologies, which is what the Green Revolution set out to do. Production systems are viable only as far as the ecosystems which support them. The governing influence must flow from the ecosystem to the production system. When ecological relations are unbalanced the very existence of the production system is threatened.

Basic Goods through Appropriate Technology

Several critics have argued that proponents of appropriate technology often ignore social relations of production and that they have a naive view of the exercise of political power. Critics have maintained, quite correctly, that appropriate technology will not come to pass unless there is the control of power to make it happen [6,7]. However, I shall argue that the view of politics first and technology later, or vice versa, is an obstacle to the progress of appropriate technology. A prior knowledge of the economics and know-how of appropriate technology is an essential part of the politics of transformation. This is particularly true of the political efforts in the Third World for satisfying basic human needs.

Earlier in this paper I gave several examples of how the choice of production forces influences social relations of production. A campaign against the development of a particular set of production forces or of a technology has a much greater likelihood of success if an alternative technology can be shown to exist that can do the job as well or better. Economic activity based on low budget appropriate technology can provide material security and an economic surplus to support the politics of economic transformation. Concrete examples of the massive employment-creating potential of appropriate technology will show that persistent unemployment is not due to the lack of, but rather to the inappropriate use of existing capital. This may help in mobilizing the vast armies of the unemployed. Similarly, a knowledge of the ecological relations of appropriate technology may help bring together environmentalists and those primarily interested in the politics of economic transformation. Finally, I shall argue the goals of a basic goods economy, to provide jobs and to satisfy the basic needs of the entire population in an ecologically sustainable fashion, become feasible only if they are expressed in terms of the economics and know-how of appropriate technology.

Given the knowledge that we now have of appropriate technologies in food and energy production, building construction, health-care, and communication, and of the regional resource potential of the tropical and semi-tropical environments, a claim can be made that it is possible to provide basic goods adequately for the masses in the Third World in an ecologically sustainable way. Obviously there are limits as to how large this population can be. Interestingly, there is increasing evidence that the basic quality of life may be an important factor in regulating birth rates. Countries such as Cuba, Taiwan, and Sri Lanka which are somewhat egalitarian in the provision of basic human needs have achieved significant declines in birth rates [21].

Some have argued that the negative social and ecological consequences of the Green Revolution are a necessary price we need to pay to stave off world hunger. This argument is false because there is a real and viable alternative to modern methods of the Green Revolution, namely the soft path techniques of organic farming [26]. High yielding varieties which require large quantities of fertilizer respond quite well to organic nutrients. Unfortunately, reliable statistics needed for calculating the potential for producing organic manure in the developing world are missing. But as a conservative estimate, waste materials of animal, plant and human origin can supply 6-8 times more nutrients than the current consumption of chemical fertilizer in these countries. The need for external application of fertilizer can also be reduced through the inclusion of legumes in the crop rotation. The control of weed and pests can be accomplished through the planting of hardier varieties, mechanical weeding, crop rotations, and adoption of biological methods of pest control [26]. Organic farming reduces degradation of the land and soil erosion by improving soil structure, which in turn reduces the need for more fertilizer to compensate for the loss of productivity due to soil erosion. Organic farming is ecologically sound, costs far less than conventional farming, and is equally productive. A sound knowledge of the methods and potential of the productive forces of organic farming is a necessary part of the political effort to alter the social relations of food production in the Third World.

A major factor in the scarcity of basic foods in the Third World is the pattern of land-use where large acreages are under cash crops for export and under feedcrops for livestock [16]. Foreign exchange earned from export crops is largely used to finance non-basic luxury consumption of the upper classes. Where land is scarce, it is a wasteful practice to use land resources for growing feedcrop for livestock. A single pound of meat requires an average consumption of approximately ten pounds of grain and soy as feed. A hectare of land growing feedcrop for chickens can supply the minimum daily protein requirements of 1430 people. However, if soy was grown on the same area for direct consumption, the land can provide the minimum daily protein requirements of 22,700 people. Furthermore, non-meat sources such as dairy and plant food can provide all of man's protein needs. Plant foods constitute incomplete sources of protein. However, complete protein can be obtained by combining legumes and grain in the diet, a principle known as protein complementarity and practiced throughout the world's cultures [15].

In the provision of energy as a basic good, it is important to follow the principle of end-use analysis based on the Second Law of Thermodynamics. The point of end-use analysis is to match the source of energy to the ultimate use in terms of type, quantity, and geographic location. For village-level applications, which for the most part require only low-grade energy, there are many promising and appropriate technologies. These include solar, wind, water, biogas, animal, and pedal power [5,27]. The production of electricity from photovoltaic cells is an expensive, sophisticated technology. The more promising use of solar energy in the rural areas of the Third World is in cooking and heating water in homes and hospitals. The best use of wind power is pumping water for irrigation and for domestic use. Water can be pumped into elevated tanks whenever wind is available and stored there for use when needed. Small water wheels can be used to grind grain and drive small machines. Even small-scale hydro electric generation is quite feasible in developing countries. Units are now available which can produce 10 kilowatts of electricity from a head of 13 feet and a flow of 120 gallons a second [5: p. 154].

A most promising technique of energy production is the methane gas digester. When organic matter is allowed to decompose anaerobically (without oxygen) it release methane, a clean combustible gas. And spent solids of the original manure make an excellent fertilizer. This technology is fairly scale-neutral and can be built on a small scale at a household, farm, or at a village level. The smallest economic size generates about 60 cft per day. The smaller plants may cost anywhere from $60 to $250 U.S. dollars [5: pp. 182-83]. A large plant which produces 5000 cft per day can be built for a cost of 41,000 Indian ruppees and can employ five people per plant. If 21,150 such plants are dispersed over a large geographical region, they will generate over six million megawatt hours of energy, will produce 230,000 tons of nitrogen per year as a by-product, and will employ 13,750 people for a total capital cost of RS 1070 million. On the other hand, a modern coal-based fertilizer plant designed to produce 230,000 tons of nitrogen per year will actually consume 0.1 million megawatt hours of energy and will employ only 1000 people at a total capital cost of RS 1200 million [20: p. 238]. Apart from supplying fertilizer and clean energy by recycling waste, the methane technology clearly shows that unemployment is not caused by a shortage of capital but by the inappropriate use of existing capital. Therefore, technologies such as methane generation are an integral part of the politics of the struggle for jobs and basic goods.

Conclusion

The concept of K-biased innovations developed in this paper can be applied to investigate at least three sources of bias in innovations: technological, social and ecological. The course of development of production forces in society depends on the nature of entrepreneurial innovation. Therefore, the study of innovation bias is important to understanding the evolution of production forces. Existing social relations of production will influence the pattern of investment in research and in the development of innovations. By an appropriate choice of factor proportions in innovations, production forces can be developed so as to reflect the existing relations of production. In fact, biased innovations are a basic mechanism employed for the continued reproduction of social relations. Therefore, the study of innovation bias is important to understanding the process by which social relations of production are maintained. The analytics of K-biased innovations are useful for looking at technological, social, and ecological aspects of appropriate technology. Since the production and delivery of basic goods in the poor countries of the third world is feasible only in the context of appropriate technology, the concept of K-biased innovations becomes central to the emerging new directions in development theory.

philosophic and sentimental sectors...It is fairly obvious that the social organization of a people is not only dependent upon their technology, but is determined to a great extent, if not wholly by it, both in form and content" (White:1959:19; Legros:19:1:26:55).

Following the theoretical perspective of White, the supporters of the theory of cultural evolution assert that the transference of technology from the developed to the less-developed countries (LDC) leads to the development of "dominant" and "dependent" cultures. The dominant cultures, it is held, are thermodynamically more versatile; they respond more effectively to different types of environment and they are likely to drive out less-developed cultures. Because of its technological superiority, they find that "Western culture is not only extending its dominance over much of this planet, but is also attempting to extend into outer space as well" (Kaplan:1960:73). Following the same line of thought, A. B. Singham and Nancy Singham argue that presently the world is dominated by two technological-cum-military super states which seek to dominate the cultures of technologically weaker societies. According to them, "the global system is dominated by a converging Euro-American cultural system which shares common technology and common concern to control and dominate the weaker cultural systems, despite different forms of economic and social organization in the two powerful super states" (Singham:15:3:263). They accept and apply Roseneau's concept of "linkages" between a national-political system and international politics and stress that such linkages also exist between the cultures of different societies. According to his definition of linkage, "any recurrent sequence of behavior that originates in one system is reacted to another" (Roseneau:1969:45). Roseneau divides linkages into three categories: the first is "penetrative", where "one polity serves as participant in the political process of another". The second is "reactive" which results in response to "behavior undertaken by the former", and finally he mentions "emulative" wherein the so-called "diffusion" or "demonstration" (Roseneau:1969:46) effect takes place. Although the Singhams place greater emphasis on the penetration of weaker by more powerful cultural systems, I believe, that in the context of socio-cultural changes taking place in the societies of the Third World, the penetrative and emulative linkages are equally significant. This kind of situation is likely to create a dominant and dependent relationship between the two cultural systems. The countries of the Third World are not only dependent on the advanced industrialized societies for the transfer of the latest technology which may come through government agencies or private business, (Watkins:34:1974), they are also intellectually indebted to these societies for the supply of the latest information in the sciences, management, the social sciences and the humanities. Indeed, researchers stress that the Third World falls on "the 'periphery' of the world's intellectual system", and industrialized nations are still "in control of the means of distribution of knowledge..." (Altbach:1970:83; Bodenheimer:15:1970).

In the context of the existence of dominant and dependent cultural systems, it is suggested that with the transference and diffusion of technology from the West, the Western culture and particularly its Anglo-American variant, with its superior scientific and technological knowledge, is likely to become the model on which the behavior patterns and socio-political organizations of non-Western cultures are likely to be built. It is believed that cultural norms, values and institutional structures originating from the metropolitan societies are likely to prevail over the normative and institutional structures existing in the less-developed countries.

The nature of the relationship between the cultures of the European and the Third World countries will be a subject of continuing debate and speculation. It is agreed, however, that transference and diffusion of technology into the LDCs is likely to erode the traditional values and attitudinal patterns and create new sets of aspirations and behavior patterns on the part of individual members of this society.

Focus of the Study

This study is concerned with the interrelationship between specific components of modern technology and the development of certain attitudinal patterns on the part of a selected group of individuals. I must stress that we are looking mainly at the diffused feelings, values and perceptions of our respondents rather than their actual behavior patterns. This socio-psychological approach of placing emphasis on attitudinal and ideological aspects of social change is as much a part of social inquiry as is the emphasis on the organizational and institutional aspects of a culture. Furthermore, although the changes in the respondents' attitudinal patterns are not being measured in terms of their experience in the operation of a system of production, nevertheless, their experience of going through modern educational institutions subjects them to a rationally organized pattern of authority. Bureaucracies and production systems, as well as modern educational institutions, are what Peter Berger *et al* have termed the centers of "human engineering". Even when the use of dichotomous concepts like "modern" and "traditional" are subject to serious scholarly criticism, it can hardly be denied that personalized use of such technological components as radios, televisions, autos, newspapers, etc. is likely to cause fundamental changes in a person's social and political outlook.

Most of the studies dealing with diffusion of innovations in political science focus on the "communication of a new idea in social system over time" (Gray:1973:1175; Warner:5:1974, Walker:1969:880-889). It is often the anthropologist who studies how the introduction of the components of new technology in a particular society brings about changes in the cultural norms and the structure of that society. Diffusion of consumption-based components of technology is a complex phenomenon which should have profound attitudinal implications for the individuals living in the societies of the Third World. It has been frequently observed that an increased pace of urbanization, higher rate of literacy, higher degree of media exposure and so on lead to the formation of modern outlooks in an individual or generally result in the development of a mobilized society. The interrelationship between the adoption of specific sets of modern technology and the consequent change in the socio-political orientations have been only infrequently looked into (Lerner:1958).

In relation to attitudinal patterns, political predispositions and values, we are especially interested in testing some of the theoretical assumptions developed in the literature dealing with liberal democratic theory. A group of scholars led by S. M. Lipset find high correlation between economic development and the successful operation of democracies. They hold that economic affluence and stable democracies go together (Lipset:1959:1963; Cutright:1969; Huntington and Nelson:1976). Another group led by G. A. Almond and S. Verba believe that a democratic political system is the product of a participant political culture, which in turn is based upon specific traits of personality of the individual member of the society. Persons with a high level of political efficacy, achievement orientations, trust in public officials, willingness to become involved in politics, etc. would be termed as individuals with democratic predispositions (Almond and Verba:1970:8-44). In the context of the recent introduction of the component of modern technology as well as democratic institutions in India, we would here specifically focus on the development of (1) personal competence as demonstrated by achievement orientation, (2) its relationship to the development of democratic predispositions, (3) the growing sense of party identification and (4) the basis of political alienation in a fast-changing society.

Setting and Research Procedure

This study was conducted in Jullundur City of Punjab, one of the three largest cities of the state. It is the headquarters of the district and the seat of the administration. The city is located on National Highway One which connects it with Amritsar at the one end and New Delhi at the other. In terms of literacy Jullundur district ranks second in the state (Government of Punjab:1971).

Although an overwhelming majority of the people still live in the older part of the city studded with *Mohallas* and crisscrossing narrow lanes and bylanes, nevertheless, since 1948 there has been a steady increase in the outward movement of the inner city population into suburban areas.

Since 1946 there has also taken place a radical change in the economy of the city. From a service and trading town, Jullundur has become a very important center of industry and commerce. Besides sporting goods, the city has several medium and small-scale industrial units engaged in the manufacture of surgical instruments, motor parts, rubber goods, engineering goods, brass and chromium sanitary fittings and electrical goods. There are various indicators of the increased industrialization of the city and the district. Census data indicate that only 50% of the population of the district is classified as agriculturists or farm workers, and the ratio must be much lower for the city. Other factors which would indicate the importance of industries to the city are the facts that the three most imported commodities in the city are iron, coal and raw materials for sporting goods, and the three most exported commodities are motor spare parts/electrical goods, iron bars/agricultural implements, and sporting goods. In recent years the emphasis in manufacturing has been shifting from sporting goods to electrical goods, sanitary fittings and farm machinery.

Furthermore, in the past decade the city has witnessed the emergence of several new networks of communication. It has become the center of the vernacular newspaper industry of the state as well as of book publishing and it has its own television and radio stations. There are twenty cinema houses showing both Indian and foreign movies.

The city's population has also been exposed to several modern organizational techniques as well as methods of mass mobilization. There is keen competition between the Congress (1) and the Jana Sangh (now called B.J.P.) for capturing the local and the state elective offices, and both the parties have been highly successful in setting up branches and party caucuses in each ward of the city. Besides the Congress and the B.J.P., the Communist, the Socialist and the Akali parties also maintain their district headquarters in the city.

With the introduction of the electorate system, the rise of several centers of political activity within the city, and the unionization of teachers, industrial workers, students, editors, office employees, traders and several other sectors of the local community, traditional loyalties based upon ascriptive ties of caste have been considerably weakened and eroded.

Jullundur city is also a well-known center of higher education. Besides having the regional campus of the Guru Nanak Dev University, it also has twelve colleges providing degrees in liberal arts, sciences, native medicines, engineering, teacher training, physical education and several other disciplines.

The institutions providing college-level education in the community are of three types:

1) Denominational colleges (called private colleges) run by the Hindu and Sikh sectarian organizations,
2) Government colleges, run by the state government, and
3) Exclusively women's colleges, run by sectarian organizations.

For a fair representation of different segments of the student population, an eight-page structured questionnaire was administered to the first-year (freshman) and the third-year (graduating) classes of all the colleges. At the request of the college officials, the questionnaire was administered to all the students present on a specific day and during the class hour. The completed questionnaires were collected by the author at the end of the class hour. This procedure resulted in the collection of 2,500 usable questionnaires. This survey was conducted in the Fall term of 1979.

The students are fairly representative of the different segments of the youth population: about 79% are between the ages of 18 and 20, 19% fall in

Sangh) and the Akali Dal (party). The two Communist parties, the CPI and the CPI (M), also enjoy considerable support in the state (Brass:1975; Wallace:1967; Nayar:1968; Baxter:1969). From among the three major parties of the state, the Congress (I) is the one which is the most polyglot party. It draws support from all the segments of the state population as well as from the different geographic regions of the state. Despite the temporary defection from the Congress of some of the influenctial leaders like Sawaran Singh (I), Mrs. Indira Gandhi has been very successful in building the level of support for her party which the undivided Congress party enjoyed in the state. It is also her faction of the Congress party which inherited the organizational structure associated with the older Congress party.

Thus the Punjab unit of the Congress (I) has been able to maintain its traditional image of a party committed to secular politics and to the ideology of democratic socialism. Despite Mrs. Indira Gandhi's arbitrary style of operation and her resorting to the emergency rule of 1975, the Congress party in the state is still able to project an image of political moderation and pro-democratic orientations.

Bharatiya Janata Party (B.J.P.) is the successor to the Jana Sangh, a party formerly supported primarily by the urban Hindus. However, Jana Sangh's experience as a unit of the Janata party, the trials and tribulations of its leadership during the emergency rule of 1975, the gain of administrative experience in the national government, and its close association with J. P. Narayan all seem to have brought about considerable transformation both in its support base and in its ideological orientations. From an ideology of Hindu chauvianism with an emphasis on Bharatiya culture, Hindi language and militant anti-Pakistan foreign policy, it has moved to non-communal, non-sectarian and a mixture of pragmatic pro-Gandhian policies. In one of its recent policy statements it emphasized its commitment to "Gandhian socialism, adding that it was the same as the decentralized economic order propounded by Jaya Prakash Narayan" (*Statesman Weekly:*1981). In foreign policy it seeks an accommodation with Pakistan. The party has also demonstrated a healthy civil libertarian and pro-democratic stance. These developments have enhanced the chances of its wider acceptance among the low caste Hindus and the minorities where it has been traditionally weak.

The Akali Dal (party) is an avowedly and militantly particularistic organization; it claims to be the exclusive and sole spokesman of the Sikhs who constitute a solid majority in the State of Punjab (Nayar:1960). The Akali Dal is closely associated with the educational, cultural and religious life of the Sikhs. It is the Akali party which has a monopoly over the S.G.P.C. (Sharomani Gurdwara Prabhandhak Committee—the peak management body for the Sikh temples). The S.G.P.C. not only exercises control over the Sikh temples but also has a huge revenue which comes from offerings and donations made by the Sikh devotees. Akali Dal, through its skilful use of the S.G.P.C. funds, continues to manage several Sikh educational, cultural and religious institutions. Thus, the Sikh denominational schools, colleges and other societies not only employ Sikh intellectuals and party workers but also try to create a distinct subnational identity among the Sikhs. Although a small section of the Akali Dal still supports the demand for the establishment of a theocratic Sikh State in Punjab, a large majority of its members seem to have accepted the existing political system as is evident from their vigorous participation in the political process at the state and the national levels.

The Communist movement has also been able to build some significant support in some sectors of the Punjabi society. The Communist Party of India (CPI) and the Communist Party Marxist (CPIM) both seem to appeal to the same segments of the state population. The organizational leadership of both the Communist parties is drawn from the Jat Sikhs while their support base includes both the Jat and non-Jat Sikh peasant farmers. Recent efforts of the Marxists have helped the party to gain some foothold among the low castes, especially among the untouchable Hindus. In Punjab, the Communist movement is primarily rural based, so it has not been very successful in enlarging its support in the cities. Despite the repeated assertions of the Communist parties that they want to work within the framework of the democratic system, both the parties in the minds of the public are identified with a revolutionary ideology aimed at the establishment of a classless and stateless society.

Although political parties have become important vehicles of social mobility and status change, in Punjab the leadership among the four major political parties is dominated by the upper castes. In recent years the parties have also become very important instruments for political entrepreneurs to amass personal wealth and power. Although occasionally a politician plays the role of a broker between the citizens and the administration, he also uses his political position to advance his own interests or the interests of his own clientele. In the words of one of the observers, "These free-looters [politicians] have only two objectives—'plunder and power', power not in the sense of ability to transform societies, but the power a bully wants, the 'power' to patronize one person, to terrorize others" (Shouri:1980:509). This may be an overstatement of the politicians' and parties' role within the context of Punjabi society, but, there is little doubt that the party leaders, referred to aptly as the "half-educated, money-making simpletons", (Thapar:1980:497) are guided by pragmatism rather than ideological goals despite their use of populistic rhetoric. They represent India's mass political culture.

Party identification is looked upon here as our respondents' preference for attachment to a specific party. It is psychological preference for rather than formal membership in a political organization (Campbell, Converse:1964). Through a specifically designed question we asked our respondents to choose from a list of several parties the one which they liked most and which they thought would be best for the country. Table 4 gives the breakdown of our respondents' preferences.

This survey was conducted on the eve of the 1980 polls when there was a major shift of voters from the former Janata Party to Mrs. Indira Ghandi's Congress party. Almost 36 per cent of the respondents are classified here as in-

Table 4

Frequency Distribution of Party Preference

Party	%
Congress (I)	34.75
Bharatiya Janta Party (BJP)	19.42
Communist Parties	4.35
Akali Dal	4.55
Independents and Others	8.05
Like No Party	28.08
Total	100.00

dependents or people who did not like any one of the political parties. The rest of the respondents clearly represent the party regulars or the hard core of supporters of the B.J.P., Akali Dal and the Communists. Despite a shift of public opinion in favor of Mrs. Indira Ghandi and a poor performance by her opponents, this group of young adults were able to maintain their loyalties to their respective political parties.

The Akali Dal here shows a much lower level of support among the youth than its statewide level of support would warrant. One can offer two interrelated explanations. First, this study was conducted in an urban area where the B.J.P. and the Congress party have traditionally enjoyed greater support than any other political party, including the Akali Dal. Secondly, this was the period when the Akali Dal was plagued with open factional fights and its leadership was bitterly engaged in a public mudslinging campaign against each other. This has seriously damaged its public image. In contrast, Mrs. Indira Gandhi's Congress party offered the image of a united party led by a charismatic and effective political leader of national reputation. These developments seem to have cut into the support for the Akali party.

Party Identification and Level of Exposure to Technology

Political parties, though primarily vehicles for capturing political power, also adopt a public posture of representing certain political ideas, values and programs. They adopt different symbols and make different types of public pronouncements so as to present a systematic view of the policies which they intend to follow and the methods which they will use to attain certain specific goals if and when they come to control political institutions. Parties do socialize the citizens, but they also attract the citizens with their ideological images. Such images and political predispositions of individuals seem to interact and reinforce the party identities. It appears that there exists a kind of pull and push relationship between the ideological images of a party and an individual's political predispositions.

With the exception of the two Communist parties, the rest of the parties represent political moderation, support for the status quo, and thus a commitment to a liberal democratic model. Findings reported in Table 5 seem to indicate a positive relationship between a higher level of exposure to modern technology and the political moderation represented by the Congress and the B.J.P. Both the Congress party and the B.J.P. represent pro-system orientation and a democratic stance and both score high on our scale of exposure to technology. The Communists are generally committed to political radicalism, and they come at the bottom of the scale of exposure to modern technology. Thus, the findings presented here basically confirm that a higher degree of exposure to and possession of the components of modern technology is likely to lead to greater political moderation and support for the status quo.

Table 5

Party Identification Cross-Tabulated with
Guttman Scale of Exposure to Technology

Level		Congress	B. Janata Party	Communist	Akali	Independent and Others	Like No Party
(High)	9	11.07	7.97	3.74	9.62	8.81	11.88
	8	7.87	7.76	3.74	.96	11.92	5.36
	7	11.93	10.06	5.60	6.73	9.84	14.78
	6	8.00	6.08	13.08	8.65	6.74	7.10
	5	6.77	9.43	.93	3.85	9.33	7.68
	4	11.69	12.58	19.63	6.73	8.29	11.16
	3	23.27	22.01	21.50	21.15	19.17	18.41
	2	15.62	18.03	22.43	36.54	18.13	20.29
(Lowe)	1	3.68	6.08	9.35	5.77	7.77	3.34
		100.00	100.00	100.00	100.00	100.00	100.00
		(813)	(477)	(107)	(104)	(193)	(690)

$X^2 = 11.286$ @ 40 d.f. $p < .0001$

It is possible to suggest that the person possessing a larger number of components of modern technology may actually belong to well-to-do segments of the society and thus a high level of political moderation may well be the product of a person's social status rather than his level of exposure to modern technology. The interrelationship between higher income and political moderation is frequently recognized by scholars (Lipset:1963), and it may well be offered as an alternative explanation of political moderation in this situation. Our data, however, are unable to provide a definitive support for this proposition. A cross-tabulation of father's occupation and party identification does not show any positive relationship. On the other hand, while the B.J.P. draws support from the uppercaste Hindus and the Akalis from the Jat Sikhs, the Congress party draws its support from all the sectors of the Punjabi society. Only the Communist parties are predominantly dependent upon the rural votes and urban poors, with some significant base among the untouchables.

Parties and Political Attitudes

Pull and push relationships between the parties and individual citizens can be demonstrated by the image of a party and the political predispositions of the respondents. Political radicalism and an anti-system stance are the common characteristics of the Communist parties despite their assertions to the contrary. On the other hand, as stated above, both the Congress (I) and the B.J.P. project images of political moderation. The findings reported in various parts of Table 6 demonstrate that even though a very large number of respondents display positive orientations toward revolutionary change, it is the Communist who express the highest degree of support for the use of revolutionary methods to change the socio-political settings of the country. On the other hand, the youth showing preference for the B.J.P. demonstrate the highest level of support for the Gandhian methods of peaceful and non-violent socio-political changes. Needless to say, almost equally strong preference for peaceful social change is shown by the supporters of the other non-Communist parties. These preferences for the use of either violent or peaceful methods may be simply expressions of diffused and generalized political predispositions, but their stable identification with a moderate or a radical party may eventually translate such predispositions into strong ideological commitments.

Rejection of peaceful methods of social change in favor of revolutionary change may be the result of a person's social origin or the consequence of the socialization process, as I have suggested in another study (Malik:1980). The process and pace of technological change as well as the level of exposure to the components of modern technology may be the other dimension which leads to the development of either political moderation or radicalism among the youth. An analysis of our data also shows that it is the youth originating from the rural area, who has recently migrated to urban centers of population and who has been suddenly exposed to the life style projected through modern components of technology, who is more prone to prefer revolutionary rather than peaceful methods of socio-political change.

In our effort to find a relationship between parties and political attitudes, we asked a series of questions in order to probe into the youth's attitudes towards democracy. Such questions submitted to the respondents dealt with both the normative and operational aspects of democracy in India. On the basis of these questions, we formulated a five-item democracy in India. When we cross-tabulate the youth's preferred party with the scale of democracy, we observe the emergence of attitudinal consistency which agrees with the findings reported in the preceding pages. An analysis of the data presented in Table 7 clearly indicates strong interrelationships between the type of party preferred and the respondent's degree of political moderation. The highest ranking on the scale of democracy is achieved by the Congress (I), Bharatiya Janata Party and the Akalis, while the Communists fall on the other end of the scale. This pattern is further reinforced when we analyze the responses of the youth to the specific questions related to their normative commitment to democracy. We

Table 6a

Preferred Party and the Use of Revolutionary
Methods to Change the Society

Need for Revolutionary Methods	Congress	B. Janata Party	Communist	Akali	Independent and Others	Like No Party
Agree	60.56	58.61	85.84	62.83	60.78	58.95
Disagree	33.41	38.52	10.62	31.86	35.78	32.92
No Opinion	6.03	2.87	3.54	5.31	3.44	8.23
	100.00	100.00	100.00	100.00	100.00	
	(862)	(488)	(113)	(113)	(204)	(729)

$X^2 = 52.45$ @ 10 d.f. $p < .0001$

Table 6b

Preferred Party and Gandhian Methods to
Solve the Problems of India

Gandhian Methods to Solve the Problems	Congress	B. Janata Party	Communist	Akali	Independent and Others	Like No Party
Agree	72.93	73.08	33.33	61.25	61.39	65.11
Disagree	20.42	22.77	60.19	31.86	31.19	27.34
No Opinion	6.65	4.15	6.48	6.19	7.42	7.55
	100.00	100.00	100.00	100.00	100.00	100.00
	(857)	(483)	(108)	(113)	(202)	(728)

$X^2 = 97.40$ @ 10. d.f. $p < .0001$

discover that only 61 per cent of the Communist youth agree with the statement that democracy is the best possible form of government, while more than
80 per cent of the supporters of the Congress (I), B.J.P. and the Akali party express support for this view. There also emerge highly significant differences
(at .0001 level) between the supporters of the Communist and non-Communist
parties in their perceptions of the operation of democracy in India. Although
the supporters of all political parties express some reservations about the Indian democracy, the Communists are the most negatively oriented towards its
operation in India. Almost 80 per cent of the Communists hold that experience
shows that democracy cannot work in India, while only around 60 per cent of
the supporters of the non-Communist parties subscribe to such a view.
Expression of pride in the economic and industrial achievements of the system
is common across the party lines. However, there emerge striking differences
among the followers of different parties in their evaluation of the political
aspects of the operation of the Indian system. Only 47 per cent of the Com-

Table 7

*Cross-Tabulation of Party Identification
and Democracy Scale*

Democracy Scale	Congress	B. Janata Party	Communist	Akali	Independent and Others	Like No Party
High	.99	.65	.96	.95	.52	1.75
Medium	81.64	85.68	57.14	83.81	75.52	80.93
Low	17.37	13.67	41.90	15.24	23.96	17.32
	100.00	100.00	100.00	100.00	100.00	100.00
	(806)	(461)	(105)	(105)	(192)	(687)

$X^2 = 55.95$ @ 10 d.f. $p < .0001$

munists are willing to express pride in the system's political achievements while, in contrast, 77 per cent of the B.J.P. supporters do so.

Interestingly, there is no positive relationship between party identification and achievement scale. Contrary to the theoretical assumptions developed in the literature dealing with empirical democratic theory, followers of liberal and leftist parties are not different from each other in terms of their personal efficacy or achievement orientations. In relation to each of the items in the achievement scale we find that whereas a Communist youth rejects fatalism and does not believe that divine or governmental help is essential, on the other hand the supporters of democratic parties not only subscribe to a fatalistic view of life but also express greater reliance on divine power for personal success. There is a highly significant difference (at .001 level) between the Communist and non-Communist youth on this point. The Communist youth, however, shows a higher level of negative orientation towards the societal environment than do the other groups. A larger majority of these than of the followers of the other parties hold that one cannot succeed in India by one's own efforts; recommendations and contacts are essential for personal success. The attitudinal differences between the two groups in their perception of the job situation existing in India is significant at .0001 level.

Evidently there seems to be a development of contradictory attitudinal patterns. If the Communist youth reject divine help for personal success and do not subscribe to the fatalistic view of life, then how can it be called a less efficacious group? It appears that students affiliated with moderate political parties generally demonstrate a greater degree of commitment to the existing norms of behavior and social values which the Communist youth rejects. Political moderation, it appears, results from a blend of traditional and modern world views.

Diffusion of Technology and Alienation

It has been demonstrated that the introduction of consumption- or production-related components of modern technology is likely to bring about certain fundamental changes in the attitudes, values and norms of behavior of the individual members of a society. In the words of Samuel Huntington, "urbanization, literacy, education, mass media, all expose the traditional man to new forms of life, new standards of enjoyment, new possibilities of satisfaction. These experiences break the cognitive and attitudinal barriers of the traditional culture and promote new levels of aspirations and wants" (Huntington:1968). The introduction of modern technology and rapid industrialization are recognized as destabilizing processes. Such a process results in the breakdown of traditional values and may lead to the development of rootlessness of an individual, alienation and consequent political violence. In answer to the question, "What happens to an individual caught in the throes of intense social change?" recent empirical studies of such change have shown in detail the disintegration of a society unable to meet the challenges posed by the modernization process, (Waltz:14:2:1982, Tumbull:1972), or they have found linkages between a rapid process of social change and increased pace of political violence. This enhanced pace of political violence is attributed to the widening gap developing between the higher level of aspirations of individuals and the limited availability of means to satisfy them (Gurr:1970; Johnson:1966). It can hardly be denied that personalized use of such components of consumption-based technology as radio, T.V., auto, telephone, movies and so on is also likely to bring about drastic changes in the norms of behavior and attitudinal patterns of an individual. Not only do radio, transistors and T.V. bring the elements of the popular culture into the confines of the family, but through frequent screening of the popular movies on the T.V. the young adults are also exposed to the romantic love between young male and female adults as well as sexually suggestive scenes which have been traditionally taboo within the Indian family. Movies also depict a standard of living which is well beyond the reaches of an overwhelming majority of the citizens of India.

The constant playing of popular music on radio and the depiction of unattainable life on T.V. and in movies are likely to erode traditional norms of behavior and create new sets of aspirations and expectations among the youth which the Indian polity is unable to meet. This gap between the rising expectations and aspirations of the youth population and the limited capabilities of the system to meet such demands, as stated above, should lead to political alienation and a tendency toward violence. My concern here is to see the interrelationship between a person's exposure to modern technology, alienation, and support for revolutionary methods of social change. There is no dearth of definitions of the concept of alienation; it is generally assumed to be a condition of powerlessness, self-estrangement, political ineffectiveness and disorientation towards the political system (Schwartz:1973; Finifter:64:1970). In order to operationalize the concept of alienation, we constructed a five-item scale[2] based upon five questions which try to probe into our respondents' level of political efficacy as well as their attitudes toward the political system. An analysis of the frequency distribution on the scale of alienation demonstrates

Table 11

Alienation and the Identification with the Types of Heroes

Level of Alienation		Pop. Culture	Types of Heroes			Other
			Political Leaders	National/ Secular	Religious Leaders	
High	1	36.61	37.35	35.36	41.08	29.01
	2	55.52	55.06	58.94	53.03	61.11
Low	3	7.87	7.59	5.70	5.98	9.88
		100.00	100.00	100.00	100.00	100.00
		(254)	(316)	(526)	(1222)	(162)

$X^2 = 16.31$ @ 8 d.f. $p < .05$

modern technology. In short, the pace and level of exposure to modern technology seem to have a direct impact on a person's perceptions of his own competence as well as on the societal environment in which he lives.

Conclusions and Discussions

An examination of the interrelationship between the diffusion of technology and political predispositions generally shows that a higher level of exposure to technology leads to the development of an attitudinal profile supportive of democratic polity. However, the ultimate direction of such a development is not clear. Even if we do not subscribe to technological determinism, we can hardly deny that the use of consumption-based technology is eroding traditional values and leading to the development of new expectations, demands and norms of behavior. One can discern the development of "penetrative" and "emulative" linkages between the dominant and dependent cultures. In the context of the Indian situation, the dominant culture is represented by Anglicized-Westernized elites who constitute India's bureaucracy, economic planners, intellectual establishment and national rulers (Weiner:1965). It is this group, however dispersed and diversified, which sets the cultural norms, value orientations and policy goals for the polity. They occupy the center of Indian politics and society. There is a tendency on the part of the common man to idealize Anglicized and Westernized Indians. State and local politicians, who represent India's mass political culture, can hardly disguise their eagerness to accept a westernized Indian as their model of behavior. "If they cannot adopt his values and life style in their own lives, they would like very much for their children to emulate him. The image of a Westernized-Anglicized Indian as an ideal to emulate has been reinforced by television, movies, magazines and newspapers" (Malik:28:1982:29).

The introduction of democratic institutions in India, as is well-known, is not the result of an internal groundswell. It was the Western-educated and Anglicized elite which made a deliberate choice for democracy over others forms of government. It has been well put that "Indians struggled against Englishmen for the right to run a British system in India" (Field:1980:347). These political elites believed that through the introduction of universal franchise and consequent mass political participation, a traditional society based upon an ascriptive oligarchic structure would transform itself into an egalitarian and open society. The spread of mass media and widespread exposure to modern technology would help in the internalization of democratic norms and values and would lead to the development of egalitarian political culture. The findings reported in the preceding pages demonstrate that values associated with the dominant elite culture are gradually penetrating the subjective structure of the young adult's consciousness. A higher level of exposure to modern technology tends to pull a person in the direction of political moderation, and thus he tends to identify himself with the political parties seeking only gradual and moderate changes in the socio-political structure of the country. In this way, we find a close interrelationship between the level of exposure to technology and the development of what G. Almond and S. Verba have referred to as the trait of participant political personality. This should support the development strategy adopted by the Westernized political elite who seek gradual, though steady, change in the traditional structure of Indian society.

If, on the other hand, we take our scale of exposure to technology as an index of a person's class or status in the society, it will support S. M. Lipset's proposition of the existence of close relationships between material affluence and democracy. According to Lipset, "Weber may have been right when he suggested that modern democracy in its clearest form can occur only under capitalist industrialization" (Lipset:1963:28). And he further adds that "the more well-to-do a nation, the greater the chances that it will sustain democracy" (Lipset:1963:31). If this position is accepted, then the traits of participant political culture as presented above should be considered as the expression of the values associated only with the upper strata of Indian society. In this situation it could be asserted that the young respondents originating from the well-to-do families of provincial towns and cities are quickly acquiring the values of the culturally dominant elites. In this way one can discern the development of linkages between the national elites and the provincial and local elites. Will it be more plausible thus to provide a class-based explanation of socio-political implications of diffusion of technology? It could be argued, for instance, that in terms of the introduction and popularization of consumption-based technology, the goal of national elites in India is not so much to create and reinforce a participant political culture as it is to emulate and reproduce Western life style in India. Democracy has not been successful in eradicating poverty nor has it been able to bridge the income gap existing between the well-to-do upper strata living in alluence and the lower strata of India living in abject poverty. The benefits of the development strategy adopted by the political elites have not been equally distributed within the society (Sharma:1973; Frankel:1971). Even the most ardent exponents of India's democratic system recognize that "three decades of democratic experience, with intensely contested local, state and national elections, have socialized the Indians, regardless of their position in the the social hierarchy, into a *common* political citizenship across the traditional divides. But existence of such citizenship into economic field whereby...irrespective of his place in the social hierarchy an individual would be able to claim the right to economic advancement and distributive justice has yet to take place'' (Somjee:1979:8). In the presence of widespread poverty both in the urban and rural areas it could be argued that westernized elites are not as interested in creating social equality by removing poverty as they are in molding their lives on the life style existing in more affluent societies. In this respect the leadership existing both in the elite and in mass political cultures seem to have common goals, and they keep reinforcing each other's position. Recent studies of rural and urban communities demonstrate that political power rests in the hands of the upper castes. ''In occupational terms, they are the more affluent cultivators and businessmen and they are mainly from higher income brackets'' (Lele:1979:113:1981). In any ''stratified society, particularly in a society like India's when socially dominant groups also come to dominate elective and organizational positions'', (Malik:1982), they are in a position to set such policy goals which will meet their own aspirations. They are able to see that rewards flow in their direction (Gangrade:1974; Rosenthal:1977). Since the regional and local elites accept Westernized-Anglicized Indians as their role models, they are eager to accept and absorb consumption-based technology and follow the national elites in their pursuit of Western life style.

Even if we need more evidence to demonstrate conclusively the relationship between social status and political moderation in general, there is enough evidence presented in this case to conclude that a higher level of exposure to modern technology leads to the development of a pro-system orientation. These persons do not seek radical transformation of the social and economic structure of the country. They may actually aspire to join the ranks of the upper classes and emulate their life style and value system. Political moderation in this way may actually be an expression of political conservatism directed towards the maintenance of the status quo. Thus, it could be argued that the continued expansion of consumption-oriented technology is likely to further spread and strengthen the upper middle class outlook among the young citizens.

NOTES

1 *Achievement Orientation Scale* is based upon the following items:
    (1) I believe that I can obtain a job on the basis of my qualifications without any recommendation. (Agree)
    (2) I believe that everyone in our society can be successful with his own efforts. (Agree)
    (3) I believe that without the help of God a man cannot be successful in his life. (Disagree)
    (4) I believe that every individual in this country needs government help to be a success in his life. (Disagree)

(5) I believe that the course of my life has been set by my fate and I cannot change it. (Disagree)

2   *The Alienation scale* is based upon the following items:

(1) Sometimes governmental and political affairs look so complex that I am unable to understand them. (Agree)

(2) I think that other than voting there is no way whereby we can influence the governmental decision-making. (Agree)

(3) If the government officials mistreat us we are unable to do anything against them. (Agree)

(4) The Government does not care for men like me; it is influenced only by the leaders of the groups or the Capitalist class. (Agree)

(5) Even though the civil servants and the politicians of our country are incompetent and they do not deserve our trust, I am still proud of the political achievements of my country. (Disagree)

REFERENCES

AHMAD, Mujeed
    1976   "Development of Nations Through Science and Technology". *Impact of* Science on Society, Vol. 22, No. 3 (May-Sept.).
ALMOND, Gabriel and Sidney VERBA
    1970   *The Civic Culture* (Little, Brown and Co.).
ALTBACH, Philip G.
    1976   "Literary Colonialism: Books in the Third World" in Philip G. Altbach *et al* (eds.) *Prospective on Publishing*. Lexington, Mass., Lexington Press.
BAXTER, Craig
    1969   *Jana Sangh: A Biography of an Indian Political Party*. Philadelphia, University of Pennsylvania Press.
BERGER, Peter, Brigette Berger and Hansfried Kelner
    1974   *The Homeless Mind: Modernization and Consciousness*. New York, Vintage Books.
BODENHEIMER, Susanne J.
    1970   "The Ideology of Developmentalism: American Political Science's Paradigm—Surrogate for Latin American Studies". *Berkeley Journal of Sociology* Vol. XV, pp. 95-137.
BRASS, Paul R.
    1975   "Ethnic Cleavages and the Punjab Party System, 1952-1972" in M. Weiner and John O. Field (eds.) *Electoral Politics in the Indian States: Party Systems and Cleavages*. New Delhi, Manohar Book Service.
CAMPBELL, Angus, Philip E. CONVERSE, Warren E. MILLER and Donald E. STOKES
    1964   *The American Voter*. (New York, John Wiley & Sons).
CUTRIGHT, Philip
    1969   "National Political Development: Measurement and Analysis", in Charles F. Cannude and Dean E. Neubauer (eds.) *Empirical Democratic Theory* (Chicago, Markham Publishing Co.), pp. 193-209.
DESSAU, Jan
    1969   "Social Factors Affecting Science and Technology in Asia", *Impact of Science on Society* Vol. 19, No. 1 (Jan.-March.), pp. 12-23.
ELDERSVELD, Samuel J. and Bashir Uddin AHMED
    1978   *Citizens and Politics: Mass Political Behavior in India*. Chicago, The University of Chicago Press.
FINIFTER, Ada
    1970   "Dimensions of Political Alienation". *American Political Science Review* Vol. 64 (June), pp. 389-410.
FIELD, John O.
    1980   *Consolidating Democracy: Politicization and Participation in India*. New Delhi, Manohar.

FLERON, Jr., Frederic J.
    1977   *Technology and Communist Culture: Socio-Cultural Impact of Technology Under Socialism.*
            New York, Praeger.
FRANKEL, Francine
    1971   *India's Green Revolution.* Princeton, Princeton University Press.
GALBRAITH, John K.
    1971   *The New Industrial State.* New York, Mentor.
GANGRADE, K. D.
    1974   *Emerging Patterns of Leadership.* Delhi: Rachna Publications.
Government of Punjab
    1971   *Census 1971: District Census Handbook.* Chandigarh, P & S Department, Series 17.
GRAY, Virginia
    1973   "Innovation in the States: A Diffusion Study", *The American Political Science Review*,
            December.
GURR, Robert Ted
    1970   *Why Men Rebel.* Princeton, Princeton University Press.
HUNTINGTON, Samuel and Jan Nelson
    1976   *No Easy Choice: Political Participation in Developing Countries.* Cambridge, Mass., Har-
            vard University Press.
HUNTINGTON, Samuel P.
    1968   *Political Order in Changing Societies.* New Haven, Yale University Press.
INKELES, A.
    1969   "Participant Citizenship in Six Developing Countries", *American Political Science
            Review*, December.
INKELES, A. and David H. SMITH
    1974   *Becoming Modern: Individual Change in Six Developing Countries.* Cambridge, Harvard
            University Press.
JOHNSON, Chalmers
    1966   *Revolutionary Change.* Boston, Little, Brown and Co.
KAPLAN, David
    1960   "The Law of Cultural Dominance", in Marshal D. Sahlins and Elman R. Service
            (eds.) *Evolution and Culture.* Ann Arbor, University of Michigan Press.
KRISHNAN, V. N.
    1979   "Cultural Change, Technology and Indian Economic Development", *Journal of
            Cultural Economics* Vol. 3, No. 1 (June), pp. 73-84.
LANE, Robert E.
    1965   *Political Life: Why and How People Get Involved in Politics.* New York, The Free Press.
LEGROS, Dominique
    1977   "Change, Necessity, and Mode of Production: A Marxist Critique of Cultural
            Evolutionism", *American Anthropologist*, Vol. 79, No. 1 (March), pp. 26-55.
LELE, Jayant K.
    1979   "A Critique of Pluralist Illusion of Participation: The Indian Case", *Contributions to
            Asian Studies*, Vol. 13.
LELE, Jayant K.
    1981   *Elite Pluralism and Class Rule: Political Development in Maharashtrag-India.* Toronto,
            University of Toronto Press.
LERNER, Daniel
    1958   *The Passing of Traditional Society.* Glenco, IL., The Free Press.
LIPSET, S. M.
    1963   *Political Man.* New York, Doubleday & Co.
LIPSET, S. M.
    1959   "Some Social Requisites of Democracy: Economic Development and Political
            Legitimacy", *American Political Science Review* (March), pp. 69-105.
MALIK, Yogendra K.
    1979   "Party Identifications and Political Attitudes Among the Secondary School Children
            of North India", *Asia Quarterly*, pp. 259-275.

Malik, Yogendra K.
   1979   "Trust, Efficacy and Attitude Toward Democracy: A Case Study from India",
          Comparative Education Review Vol. 23, No. 3, (Oct.), pp. 433-442.
Malik, Yogendra K.
   1980   "Efficacy, Values and Socialization: A Case Study of North Indian Youth", *Political
          Science Review* Vol. 19, No. 1 (Jan.-March.), pp. 71-88.
Malik, Yogendra K.
   1982   "Politics and Power in an Urban Community of Punjab", *Indian Journal of Public Ad-
          ministration* Vol. 28, No. 1 (Jan.-March.).
Mc Clelland, David C.
   1971   "The Achievement Motive in Economic Growth" in Jason L. Finkle and Richard
          W. Gable (eds.) *Political Development and Social Change.* New York, John Wiley & Sons.
Milbrath, Lester W. and M. L. Goel
   1977   *Political Participation: How and Why Do People Get Involved in Politics.* Chicago, Rand Mc
          Nally Publishing Co.
Nayar, B. R.
   1968   "Punjab" in M. Weiner (ed.) *State Politics in India.* Princeton, N.J., Princeton
          University Press.
Nayar, Baldev Raj
   1966   *Minority Politics in the Punjab.* Princeton, N.J., Princeton University Press.
Roseneau, James (ed.)
   1969   *Linkage Politics.* New York, Free Press.
Rosenthal, Donald
   1977   *The Expensive Elite.* Berkeley, University of California Press.
Schwartz, David C.
   1973   *Political Alienation and Political Behavior.* Chicago, Aldine Publishing Co.
Sharma, H. P.
   1973   "Green Revolution in India: A Prelude to Red One?" in K. Gaugh and H. P. Shar-
          ma (eds.) *Imperialism and Revolution in South Asia.* New York, Monthly Review Press,
          pp. 77-102.
Sheth, D. L. (ed.)
   1975   *Citizens and Parties: Aspects of Competitive Politics in India.* New Delhi, Allied.
Shouri, Arun
   1980   "The State as Private Property", *Economic and Political Weekly* March 8.
Singham, Archibald W. and Nancy L.
   1973   "Cultural Domination and Political Subordination: Notes Towards a Theory of
          Caribbean Political System", *Comparative Studies in Society and History* Vol. 15, No. 3
          (June).
Somjee, A. H.
   1979   *Democratic Process in a Developing Society.* New York, St. Martin's Press.
Thapar, Romesh
   1980   *Economic and Political Weekly.*
Tumbull, Colin A.
   1972   *The Mountain People.* New York, Simon & Schuster.
Walker, J.
   1969   "The Diffusion of Innovations Among American States", *American Political Science
          Review* (Sept.), pp. 880-899.
Wallace, Paul
   1967   "The Political Party System of Punjab State: A Study of Factionalism", (an un-
          published Ph.D. dissertation, Ann Arbor, University Micro films).
Waltz, Susan E.
   1982   "Antidotes for Social Malaise: Alienation, Efficacy and Participation in Tunisia",
          Comparative Politics, Vol. 14, No. 2 (Jan.), pp. 127-147.
Warner, Kenneth E.
   1974   "The Need for Some Innovative Concepts of Diffusion of Innovation: An Examina-
          tion of Research on the Diffusion of Innovations", *Policy Sciences* 5, pp. 433-451.

WEINER, M.
   1965   "India: Two Political Cultures" in Lucian W. Pye and Sidney Verba (eds.) *Political Culture and Political Development* (Princeton, Princeton University Press).
WHITE, Leslie
   1959   Evolution of Culture. New York, Mc Graw Hill.
WILKINS, Mira
   1974   "The Role of Private Business in International Diffusion of Technology", *Journal of Economic History* Vol. 34 (March.), pp. 166-188.

Modernity and Industrial Culture of Indian Elites

DHIRENDRA VAJPEYI

University of Northern Iowa Cedar Falls, U.S.A.

I

ONE OF THE MOST salient features of the contemporary world is the tremendous transformation in science and technology.[1] The harnessing of atomic energy, the space breakthrough, the invention of cybernetic machines capable of acting as a substitute for the human brain, the approach to the practical solution of the perennial puzzles of life and heredity, due to the advances made in molecular biology and genetics, "the scientific anticipation of the probable future and its chief technological aspects (futurology) are quite indicative of the 'technologicalization' of our time". (Drucker 1957:5) Most of the industrialized countries in the West as well as less developed countries in the South have accepted that industrial development is indispensable for economic and social progress, is a prerequisite for raising levels of income and employment, 'an instrument allowing its owners to exercise social control in various forms, decisively affects modes of decision-making, and is related to patterns of alienation characteristic of alluent societies'. (Goulet 1977:11) Doubts and fears of a philosophical and practical nature have been expressed about the catastrophic consequences of technological advances on man and society.

It is also realized that technology "is no panacea for the ills of underdevelopment, even at best its promise is uncertain". (Goulet 1977:251) More specifically, criticism of industrialization in developing countries has taken two main forms: (i) industrialization has not led to a reduction in unemployment nor to a decrease in inequality, and (ii) industry has been developed to the neglect of other sectors of the economy, especially agriculture. With the introduction of technology, new roles take the place of old ones, and new expectations, sources of power and influence emerge. (Parsons 1951:513).

These changes in turn directly challenge the normative values of the industrializing society. Students of industrialism have maintained that technology strips societies and their members of their sources of meaning, undermines their view of nature, authority, and the very purpose of life. An increase in alienation is the price exacted of societies which pursue technological success competitively. Thus pursued, technology reduces the totality of human meaning to those of its elements which are amenable to problem solving. Kinship and other intimate relationships become subordinated to criteria of performance or power, pervasive 'commercialization' of friendship, of love, of procreation, of partnership. (Goulet 1977:12-13). Thus the role of values in science and technology attains a crucial importance: Whether science and technology are at all desirable for the development of human society; whether some of their characteristics are good for the progress of humanity, while others are bad, and to what extent the 'good' characteristics should be pursued to harmonize the social development of mankind with nature. (Mukherjee 1977:12).

Other questions causing anxiety all over the world are: where is this vigorous and rapid progress leading us, and in what will it ultimately result? Does it not harbor some grave dangers for man? What measures must be taken *now* to direct this progress so that it is for the good and benefit of mankind and is without negative consequences?

It has been observed that, until now, the modern democratic welfare states of the West have been able to contain the dynamics of scientific and technological change without causing serious ill effects. This is undoubtedly due to two facts: 1) from the beginning technological change was indigenous to these countries, 2) change took place gradually over the years and only recently took on an explosive momentum. The developing non-industrialized societies on the other hand, have had to launch ambitious 'century skipping' social and economic programs. They cannot afford the luxury of time and gradualness in development which typifies the now developed countries. They are caught in a dilemma like Alice in the unreal world: ''Well in our country'', said Alice, still panting a little, ''you'd generally get to somewhere else—if you run very fast for a long time, as we have been doing''. ''A slow sort of country!'' said the Queen. ''Now here, you see, it takes all the running *you* can do, to keep in the same place. If you want to get somewhere else, you must run at least twice as fast as that''. (Carrol 1965:26)

The need is for telescopic changes to take place faster than they ever did in the early development of the western countries. The long stagnation in the underdeveloped countries has solidified institutions and attitudes, and hardened resistance to change in all strata of their populations. The onslaught of modernization from outside, without the gradual transition experienced by the Western countries and in the presence of a population explosion, leads to a situation where elements of modernism are sprinkled through a society in which many conditions have remained almost the same for centuries. As Nehru said of India: ''Our country at the present moment is a very mixed country. Almost every century is represented in India: from the stone age in which some tribals live, you may say, to the middle of the twentieth century. We have atomic energy and we use also cow dung''. Researchers (Theordorsen 1953:477-484; Linton 1952:139; Hussain 1956; Muller 1970) have demonstrated that there is a certain degree of 'determinism' in the process of modernization and industrialization. The introduction of machines is expected to lead to the emergence of new social, economic, and political patterns. It will be a short-sighted and naive assumption that somehow only 'desirable' aspects of Western industrialization can be imported, and less desirable aspects can be excluded... "These patterns will resemble, in time, certain dominant patterns of Western industrialized society, which may not be rejected by any people who accept the machines of the West". (Theordorsen 1953:477)

Concerns have been expressed in the voluminous literature which ranges from serious sociological and philosophical essays to counterculture movements and antiutopian fiction dedicated within this century to the science of technology. Although some of these studies, such as the works of Jacques Ellul, (1964) Kahn and Weiner, (1967) and some others, (Polyani 1957; Ferkiss 1969; Martin 1955; Vonnegut 1967; Wright 1942; Schwartz 1971) are of extraordinary interest and are relevant to an understanding of our time. Ellul contends that technology has become a self-developing system and has introduced an irreversible cultural mutation in the evaluation of mankind, with the result that man is becoming a dependent, if not a slave, of his now autonomously growing invention.

This view is opposed by other writers, but it is interesting to observe, as in the case of Ferkiss', that the accepted basis for man's continued control of technology (technological man in place of the former industrial man) is further technological development. This is why some other students of technology, as for example McHale (1969), accept technological development as the most relevant evolutionary change in the overall biocultural evolution of mankind. The fact is that whatever one's final judgment of Ellul's views, the possible effect of such innovations as cyborgs (Clarke 1964) and the widespread use of psychosociological conditioning may eventually either bring about a general debasement of man or introduce irreversible qualitative inequalities among men and societies.

My research explores the attitudes, perceptions, opinions and beliefs of the Indian elites towards technology and modernization. Since today investment-related policy decisions in the developing countries are taken for the most part by public authorities and not by private groups, the development and growth of technology depends very much upon authoritative allocation of resources. Political observers and scholars alike have attempted to analyze, interpret, and understand the nature of this allocation system, and the motives, beliefs and values which guide and influence the political behaviors of the decision-makers or elites who occupy positions of influence and power due to ascriptive or prescriptive reasons and play a very crucial role in bringing about social and political change through structural and policy innovations. The use of political culture in comparative politics is intended to answer questions concerning the consequences of differences in attitudes, opinions, values, and sentiments which shape politics. It also emphasizes the relationship between political actions and 'particular patterns of orientations'.[2]

For the discussion of elite industrial culture in India, and since my interest is in finding out the elite attitudes, opinions and preferences only in one crucial area of policy process, I have focused on the policy culture-aspect of the system as taken from cognitive, affective and evaluative viewpoints.

II

Definition of elites, background and the Sample of the Study

Although many factors contribute to nation-building, economic growth and the political development of a country, the most crucial among them is the role of its elites who are charged with policy formulation, policy implementation and the development of popular enthusiasm in those classes which formerly played a passive part in political life. Elite orientations condition the nature and stability of the political system. Who governs, who is in charge, and why some elites have been able to lead their societies to prosperity and growth while others have failed to do so are, therefore, intriguing questions which require close analysis and attention.

Various definitions of elites have been suggested by the students who undertook comparative study of political elites, such as offered by Gaetano Mosca, Vilfredo Pareto, and Robert Michels. According to Mosca, "In all societies...two classes of people appear—a class that rules and a class that is ruled. The first class, always the less numerous, performs all political functions, monopolizes power and enjoys the advantages that power brings, whereas the second, the more numerous class, is directed and controlled by the first". (Mosca 1939:50)

A more contemporary usage, proposed by S. F. Nadel, is that an elite is "a stratum of the population which, for whatever reason, can claim a position of superiority; hence, a corresponding measure of influence over the fate of the community". (Nadel 1956:413) The concept of elite as defined by Nadel is significant in societies which are experiencing change and are in the process of modernization and development. In situations of development great emphasis is placed on new skills and techniques, and "this may mean changes in the whole notion of social superiority, and conceivably the emergence of new elites". (Nadel 1956:414)

The elite "sets standards for the whole society, its influence or power being that of a model accepted and considered worth following. It is in this sense that any established elite has the power to facilitate or hinder new developments and generally, to make new ideas acceptable to the group at large". (Nadel 1956:416).

Echoing the sentiments of Karl Marx that "the ideas of the ruling class are, in every age, the ruling ideas", Parkin observes that "those groups in society which occupy positions of the greatest power and privilege will also tend to have the greatest access to the means of legitimation". (Parkin 1971:82) He further adds that "...the extent to which values are legitimized in society is largely a function of institutional power. Values are much more likely to flow

in a 'downward' than an 'upward' direction. Consequently, moral assumptions which originate within the subordinate class tend to win little acceptance
among the dominant class. The reverse power, however, is much more marked
so that normative consensus is better understood in terms of the socialization of
one class by another rather than as independent class agreement or con-
vergence of values''. (Parkin 1971:81)

There is, at times, a total cultural dissociation between the elite and the
people. Filling the gap in developing countries are ''the middle elites, or those
individuals in the intermediate roles who are the vehicles or national interpreters of the national political culture''. (Kothari 1970:282) The idea of
'brokers' in developing political systems is based on the concept of a 'middle
status' of elites or mediators. According to Kothari, the middle elites' role is
primarily that of a communication link between the masses and the national
elites, and since the middle elites' ''style of communication and organization is
not as remote and alien as that of the higher-ups, their interpretation of
religious and caste symbols is more acceptable, and their cross-cutting between
the secular and the sacred establish them as the natural interpreters of the national political culture''. (Kothari 1970:282)

Determining Elites in India

Ever since the issue of elites has drawn the attention of researchers many
attempts have been made to classify elites. The most common indicators used
to determine the elite category have been power, wealth, and status.

A cursory review of literature on community decision-making (Aiken
1970; Bonjean 1971; Clark 1968; Jacob 1971) reveals attempts to develop 'ex-
planatory' models in this area of elite attitudes, values, and behaviors. Three
classes of factors which affect leadership decisions have been identified: (i) personality structure of a leader as it emerges through his socialization, (ii) expectations of the people around him about his social and/or political roles, and (iii)
characteristic behavioral patterns of the culture which he is part of. A leader's
decisions and actions result from interaction among these factors. This interaction produces, among many things, some conception of 'good' and 'bad',
'desirable', and 'undesirable' with regard to choices a leader has to make for
arriving at a decision. This aspect of decision-making is conceptualized as
'normative values' of leaders and is considered crucial in exploring the relationships between elite perception of issues, behavior, and career patterns.

Nadel (1956:434) distinguishes three types of elite: 1) social elites consisting of socially prominent members who have potential power, 2) governing
elites including society's political rulers who enjoy preeminence due to their
legislative and coercive authority over the most general affairs of the social and
political systems, and 3) specialized elites who are prominent members of their
own particular professions, trades or activities. These are the elites whose influence on affairs is indirect. The governing elites bargain with and respect
them. They are also called 'strategic elite' or 'managerial elite'. (1942) They
also include trade union elites, mass media leaders, and bureaucrats.

Fleron (1969) identified two classes of elites on the basis of primary institutional affiliations: 1) political elites including (a) party elites, (b) non-party elites (bureaucrats), and 2) specialized elites consisting of scientists, educators, and technicians.

For the purpose of the present study, the definition of elites was developed by combining ideas from Nadel, Fleron, Burnham, and the 'positional' and the 'reputational' techniques used in community power studies—although the 'opinion leaders' are not identical with people who are reputed to be influential: rather they are people whom the positional leaders report as actually having been sources of ideas or partners in discussions of issues. The following categories of elites were selected for the present purpose:

1. *Government*: This is considered, by some theorists, as a mere 'superstructure' serving basic economic and other interests. Others regard governmental leaders and apparatus as longstanding independent interests in themselves. Be that as it may, the legislative and executive branches play key parts in the process of policymaking, and their personnel are obviously valuable informants on the operation of the system. The legislators' role in initiating policies is clear. Hence, members of Parliament and State Legislatures were included. The time has long passed when permanent civil servants were considered mere neutral administrators carrying out mandates of the legislature and the cabinet members. The civil service plays a major and legitimate part in recommending programs and in resisting policies imposed on them which they dislike. "The bureaucracy" is thus partly an interest group in its own right and partly a body which represents wider interests outside government which it serves. Within the executive branch, top civil servants who head operating agencies and occupy key staff positions were included.

2. *Political Parties*: The role of political parties is crucial in mobilizing people and resources and in bringing about social and political change. In a developing polity such as India's they also handle the process of participation, legitimacy, management of conflict, and national integration. After independence, India's political parties, Congress, and others have been instruments for the stimulation of political consciousness and expanded participation. The party leaders are involved in 'power broker' functions for interest groups, liaison with legislators, and selection of candidates for general elections. Therefore, a decision was made to include political party chairmen, presidents and secretaries of the ruling party, and the two main opposition parties at the national, state, and district levels.

3. *The Intelligentsia*: Since the beginning of the independence struggle, political leadership and, later, political power have remained in the hands of the educated middle class, the intelligentsia. It was this group which produced the largest number of political leaders in all parties. In India this condition continues to exist, and the intelligentsia has come to enjoy exceptional influence. It has introduced into India the Western political paraphernalia of parliament, free elections, parties, platforms, economic institutions and ideologies, all of which are alien to the masses. Lawyers, teachers, writers, university administrators and student leaders are included in this group.

4. *Mass Media*: Exposure to the mass media is an important variable in large sclae, directed social change and modernization in developing societies. Since the media is a major purveyor of modern influences the learning of modern political roles (political socialization) comes in part from the mass media system. The nature and scope of the mass media differ from one country to another. In less-developed countries it reaches only to smaller audiences due to the non-availability of newspapers, magazines, radios and televisions, and the degree of government control.

The selection of which positions to study within the mass media involves the debate over 'publishers versus editors'. Ideally one would want to study both publishers and editors. Many publishers play a very passive role in relation to the content of the publications concerning themselves mostly with the levels of profits; others play a more active role ranging from keeping informed about the editorial content to closely directing that content.

For the purpose of this study an arbitrary decision was made to concentrate on editors of major national and state newspapers, and a small number of widely-reprinted newspaper columnists, and to exclude radio and television. The latter are heavily controlled by the government.

5. *Non-Associational and Public Affairs Organizations*: These were defined as organizations representing large or prestigious groups of the major caste organizations at national, state, and district levels. Also were included women's organizations, social service, and professional organizations. This is clearly a very heterogeneous category and does not constitute the kind of group with common experiences and interests. One contribution of this category is to provide perspectives on the overall system from many more vantage points. The linkages between these groups and the larger sectors previously described should help in mapping the system of communication and influence. They also have in common that they are lobbying groups, oriented to reaching government and mobilizing their constituencies.

Background and the Sample of the Study

The data were collected between January and June of 1976 at national, state, and district levels. The national elites were interviewed in Delhi and in their respective states, Madhya Pradesh, Tamilnadu, and Uttar Pradesh. The state selected for intensive study was Uttar-Pradesh and, therefore, interviews were conducted in Lucknow and the twelve districts chosen for the project.

1. *Government*: To draw a sample for the members of Parliament, I chose three geographically and politically diverse states—Madhya Pradesh, Tamilnadu, and Uttar Pradesh. Such a selection also provided a 'national' flavor to the sample. One-fourth of each state's total members in both houses of Parliament were selected on the basis of their pattern affiliation and geographical representation. The following sample emerged:

Table I

	Madhya Pradesh	Tamilnadu	Uttar Pradesh
Rajya Sabha	4	5	9
	(16)	(18)	(34)
Lok Sabha	10	10	22
	(37)	(39)	(85)
Total	14	15	31
	(41)	(44)	(94)

Total Sample = 60
(The total number of the M.P.s from respective states is in parenthesis).

At the state level, I selected the north Indian state of Uttar Pradesh for two main reasons:

1. U.P. occupies a central place in Indian politics. Its entire constitutional history has taken place without upsetting boundary changes; its culture stands as the longest available residium of interaction of all religions, culture, and traditions of India. It is the largest state in India with a population of more than 73 million in an area of 113,454 square miles. The eastern districts are among the most poverty stricken in the entire country while the western districts are economically much better off and more highly industrialized. In the rural areas, the village settlement pattern differs, with compact villages found in the western districts, groupings of hamlets in the eastern districts, and a combination of both (a cluster plus a few hamlets) in the central part. In economic development there is diversity, with some districts showing expansion while others are stagnant, and still others in decline. There are distinctions within Hindi on an East-West basis. There is crop variation with rice being more important in the East and wheat in the West. In the political sphere the state has been viewed as the national stronghold of the Congress party. It had been, until 1967, a one-party dominant state. There are many opposition parties in the state with overt differences between them in locale of strength as well as in ideology and background.

2. It has been observed that since India is a federal system and since the states are 'training grounds' for national politicians, "our very understanding of the Indian political system depends upon our assessment of patterns of development within the constituent units". "...each of the Indian states provides us with an unusual microcosm and macrocosm for studying process development. A microcosm since the states are constituent units of a larger system, and a macrocosm because the units are themselves so large that they can be studied as a total system. (Weiner 1967:3)

In U.P. twelve districts, on the basis of their socio-economic development (SED) and geographical representation, were selected for drawing a sample at state and distinct levels. Members of the Legislative Assembly (Vidhan Sabha) from the following districts were included in the sample:

Table II

Districts Selected in Uttar Pradesh

Level of SED	Eastern Region	Central Region	Western Region
High	1. Varanasi (13)	1. Kanpur (14)	1. Meerut (15)
	2. Mirzapur (7)	2. Etah (8)	2. Muzaffarnager (8)
Low	1. Gonda (12)	1. Badaun (9)	1. Almora (4)
	2. Jaunpur (10)	3. Sitapur (9)	
	3. Gorakhpur (15)		
Total	57	40	27

Grand Total = 124 (Number of members of Legislative Assembly are given in parenthesis).

At the district levels twelve Zila Pramukhs (one from each district selected in U.P.) were included in the sample.

At the national (10) and state (8) level senior members of the Civil Service directly responsible for nation-building programs were selected. Also in U.P. twelve District Planning officers were included in the sample.

Total = 226

2. *Political Parties*: At the national, state, and district levels the presidents and secretaries of the political party in power (Congress) and of the two main opposition parties were selected.

National level   =   6
State level (U.P.)   =   6
District level   =   42
   Total   54

3. *Intelligentsia*: Student leaders, lawyers, teachers, and university administrators.

National level   =   10
State level   =   10
District level   =   12
   Total   32

4. *Mass Media*: Two newspapers (one English and the other Hindi) were selected on the basis of their circulation both at the national and state levels.

National level   =   2
State level   =   2
   Total   4

5. *Non-Associational and Public Affairs Organizations*:

National level   =   20
State level   =   10

District level   =   12
       Total   42
Grand Total   358

The survey research method was used to interview the respondents. Three types of questions were used in the schedule: open ended, closed ended, and Likert-type scale to measure the attitudes and opinions of the elites. The questions asked for information not only on social backgrounds and opinions but also on the sources of information and ideas to which leaders exposed themselves, the methods they used to try to influence others, and how they were connected in networks of informal discussion and influence.

The questionnaire sought to determine values held by members of the sample in terms of their orientations and specific perceptions of social issues and problems, valued and fundamental beliefs towards egalitarianism, government outputs, role of industrialization in economic and social spheres, and in social and political change.

III

Findings

The Indian struggle for independence had both economic and political objectives. Mahatma Gandhi often said that radical, social and economic reforms are inevitable once political freedom is achieved. The idea of economic equality was interlinked with political equality. The economic ideologies of the various groups forming the Congress party during the independence movement were dominated by urban intellectuals who favored a Socialist India with emphasis on industrialization and economic growth based on Western experiences, and the Gandhians who believed in local development centered around village self sufficiency, small scale industries, and handicrafts. The Congress approach was a mixture of the beliefs of both Gandhians and westernized urban Socialist intellectuals. While they differed in strategy, both groups believed in egalitarian ideology in economic development programs and widespread ownership of the means of production. The Karachi Session of the Indian National Congress in 1931 favored, besides many other economic measures, the state control of "key industries and services and natural resources...(AICC 1955:11) When India became independent in 1947, the Congress Party reiterated its previously formulated ideas and programs in the economic sphere. India's industrial policy was enunciated by two industrial policy resolutions. The fundamental factor governing India's industrial policy has been to achieve self-reliance. India has presented both ideological and pragmatic justifications for its industrialization and mixed economy. Since independence, India's industrialization has more than trebled and Indian planners have shown preference for the public sector. (IYB 1980) The political history of India's industrialization in the last 34 years is a seesaw debate between the 'modern' and the appropriate. The short-lived Janata government promised to shift some economic priorities, and decided to move away from the heavy industry preoccupation to small-scale industry in the countryside where most Indians live. Mrs. Gandhi's government is still "floundering with regard to its industrial technology policy and continues to react to events instead of taking every opportunity to plan for the future". (1981:68) The performance of the public sector has been quite discouraging. It has shown a poor record of capacity utilization, mismanagement and lack of vision owing to the following reasons:

   (i)   Great reluctance to introduce modern management tools such as cost-benefit analysis.

  (ii)   Excessive Parliamentary scrutiny and criticism.

 (iii)   Unsatisfactory labor relations.

 (iv)   Personnel problems including apathy, risk and responsibility avoidance, delay, red tape, and lack of imagination. (Medhora 1973:17-29)

Due to the increasing lack of consensus on the nature, direction, and type of industrialization best suited to India's consumer, defense, and export needs, it is important to know about the industrial culture (cognitive, affective and evaluative) of the Indian elites who directly and indirectly influence, participate and direct policy formulation and its implementation. Such an attempt might provide us with some insights for interpreting and analysing the industrial culture of the Indian elites. "The basic notion of industrial culture is that there exists within any system a commonly held core of patterned beliefs and normative dispositions towards industrialization and technologicalization". (Drucker 1957:11)

Industrial Culture Variables

   (i)   *Evaluation of Industrial Programs, and level of Satisfaction with their performance.*

To a great extent the success of programs and policies depends on their acceptance by persons responsible for their educational diffusion and implementation. The data presented here show that a large majority of the elites did not favor a radical change in the industrial policies and programs of India. 57% of the elites at the national level and 52% at the state level reported the industrial programs in fine shape; 23% and 28%, respectively, felt that major reforms should be introduced immediately (Table III). Suggested reforms did not include any radical changes in the economic system, or in industrial policy. More efficiency and some reordering of the priorities were mentioned. Elites were, by and large, satisfied with the performance of the program. Of course, total satisfaction was not expected. Also, given the extent of criticism of public sector industries in India, the level of elite satisfaction with their performance was quite high. Only 16% of the national elites and 19% of the U.P. elites were dissatisfied with the performance of industries (Table IV).

Table III

Elite Evaluation of the Industrial Program in India
(per cent)

Elite Evaluation of Industrial Program	India	U.P.
1. Fine as it is	57	52
2. Needs immediate major reforms	23	28
3. Radically wrong, everything must change	16	18
4. Don't know	4	2
Total	100	100

Table IV

Level of Satisfaction with the Performance of Industries
(per cent)

Level of Satisfaction	India	U.P.
1. Very satisfied	40	38
2. Somewhat satisfied	30	27
3. Dissatisfied	16	19
4. Satisfied with some things but not with others	14	16
5. Don't know	--	--
Total.	100	100

(ii)   *Elite Perception of the impact of Industrialization:*
Researchers (JeQuier 1976; Stanley 1978; Goldman 1973:184-87; LaPorte
1975:393-398; Taviss 1972:606-621; Withey 1959:383-388) point out that in-
dustrialiation has too frequently been geared to satisfy the demands of upper
income groups, with consequences detrimental to employment generation, the
equitable distribution of income and social justice. It is likely, therefore, that
the farreaching consequences of technological change will not be 'evenly' felt
or experienced by the population, but rather, that various sections of the society will respond and participate differently and, therefore, benefit accordingly.
The data on India show that only 19% of the elite at both national and state
levels felt that industrialization will benefit only the rich and powerful. 31%
national and 23% U.P. elites felt that industrialization programs strengthen
the society. 36% Indian and 34% U.P. elites perceived industrialization as the
source of economic prosperity. 27% and 17% respectively thought that it will
introduce an egalitarian system, while 17% national and 21% U.P. elites felt
that crime will be increased. The differences between U.P. and national elites
are significant. (Table V)
(iii)   *Impact of Industrialization on the Value System*
The cultural and social values of a society are considered integral parts of the

innovation process. The rapid introduction of new ideas, skills, and approaches could easily erode the societal value system causing alienation, disruption, and disintegration. No elites, however, committed as they might be to modernization and change, can effectively cope with such a crisis. The elites in India were asked about their perception of the industrialization impact on the nation's value system. 49% national and 46% U.P. respondents

Table V

Elite Perception of the impact of Industrialization*
(per cent)

Industrialization	India	U.P.
1. Strengthens the Society	31	23
2. Destroys our traditional values (family, friendship authority system)	20	27
3. Economic Prosperity	36	34
4. Egalitarian System	27	17
5. Benefits only rich and powerful	19	19
6. Increases crime	17	21

* (Exceeds 100% because of multiple responses).

perceived a great deal of positive impact on the value system. Only 19% national and 20% U.P. elites saw a great deal of negative impact. (Table VI) Most of the respondents dismissed the notion that the detrimental consequences of Western Industrial experience are bound to occur in India. They did not support the 'determinist' thinking. Instead they felt that India can learn from Western experience and can avoid some of the pitfalls. Also mentioned were India's spiritual values and absence of a cutthroat "acquisitive ethos". (*Havas*)

Table VI

Impact of Industrialization on the Value System
(per cent)

Impact on Values	India	U.P.
1. *Positive Impact*		
A. A great deal	49	46
B. Somewhat	21	23
C. None	6	7
2. *Negative Impact*		
A. A great deal	19	20
B. Somewhat	5	4
C. None	0	0
Total	100	100

Table XI

Empathy and Industrialism*
(per cent)

Levels of Empathy (E)	India	U.P.	Levels of Industrialism (LI)	India	U.P.
High	82	81	High	64	62
Medium	12	14	Medium	30	32
Low	6	5	Low	6	6
Total	100	100	Total	100	100

* rE/LI = .94 (India); rE/LI = .93 (U.P.)

Exposure to Mass Media and Industrialism

Exposure to mass media is an important variable in large-scale directed social change and modernization in developing societies. In transitional societies, the learning of modern political roles (socialization) comes, in part, from later experience with the mass media system. Since the media is a purveyor of modern influences, high mass media exposure is also correlated with other variables—participation and knowledge of public affairs, support for governmental policies and actions—of modern political culture. The present data show that a high percent of Indian elites who were exposed to mass media were also supportive of industrialism in India (Table XII).

Table XII

Level of Exposure to Mass Media* and Industrialism
(per cent)

Exposure to Mass Media	India	U.P.	Level of Industrialism	India	U.P.
High	76	72	High	63	63
Medium	14	12	Medium	31	32
Low	10	16	Low	6	5
Total	100	100	Total	100	100

(* News consumption through mass media channels such as radio, newspaper, cinema, TV, magazines and journals). (rEM/LI = .92 (India), rEM/LI = .86 (U.P.)

Concept of Time and Industrialism

Time is an important, perhaps even fundamental, component of social change and development. "It is a symbolic form for organizing our experience of change and conceiving the relation between things"; (Gunnel 1970:53) "that change and time are closely linked, nearly synonymous, and to account for one is in some sense to account for the other". (Gunnel 1970:53) Attitudes toward the past, present, and future have an important influence on a receptivity to progress and on the activities which engineer change. A distinction is made between those cultures/subcultures which perceive time to be cyclical and eternally returning and those cultures/subcultures which perceive time to be linear and directed. While a mixture of both perceptions is found in most, if not all societies, 'traditional' societies are usually held to perceive time as cyclical and 'modern' societies linear. Linear time "yields the politics of expectation, the politics of collective improvement...in which the present becomes devalued for the sake of the future". Just as political culture contains elite perception and mass components, so do perspectives of cultural time. The elite perception is 'developmentalist'. It manifests "a belief that time is a helpful instrument available to man in his struggle for a better future". (Lee 1970:182) The present study found that 67% of the national sample and 64% of the state sample were modern in their perception of time in relation to modernization and social change, while 32% and 34%, respectively, were traditional or cyclical in their perception of time. The correlation between the linear concept of time and high industrialism, and cyclical time with medium and low industrialism was reported (Table XIII).

Table XIII

Modernism and Traditionalism by Sense of Time, and Industrialism*
(per cent)

Concept of Time	India	U.P.	Level of Industrialism	India	U.P.
Modern (Linear concept of time)	67	64	High	68	65
Traditional (Cyclinal Sense of time)	32	34	Medium	28	25
			Low	4	10
No Answer	1	2	---	--	--
Total	100	100	Total	100	100

* rMT/LI = .99 (India)
    rMT/LI = .96 (U.P.)

Fatalism and Industrialism

Fatalism is the belief that phenomena occur for no knowledgeable reason, and that nothing can be done to control or prevent them. God or some other moral order controls man's destiny. Fatalistic attitudes are predominantly found in traditional societies, (Vajpeyi 1979:145) have dysfunctional consequences for programs of directed change, and are a barrier to modernization. Fatalism is an 'ethos of passivity' and breeds inaction, apathy, superstition, irrational behavior, and pessimism. To assess the modernity of elite political culture, respondents were asked a series of questions related to fatalistic views of life. The data report 26% of national and 17% of state elites to be moderately fatalistic, while 53% and 56% respectively, were low on fatalism. 21% national elites and 27% U.P. elites were found to be highly fatalistic. A high correlation is found between the degree of fatalism and the industrial culture. Those elites who were highly fatalistic were low on the industrial culture and vice versa (Table XIV).

Table XIV

Elite Fatalism and Industrialism*
(per cent)

Level of Fatalism	India	U.P.	Level of Industrialism	India	U.P.
High	21	27	Low	19	21
Medium	26	17	Medium	23	20
Low	53	56	High	58	59
Total	100	100	Total	100	100

* rEF/LI = .99 (India)
  rEF/LI = .97 (U.P.)

It has been observed that politics in India represents more than a set of conflicts between groups—that it involves something far deeper: the conflict between two political cultures which have emerged since the departure of the British in 1947. As Weiner has commented:

> There thus emerged in post-independent India two political cultures operating at different levels of Indian society. One culture is in the districts. In permeates local politics, both urban and rural, local party organization, and local administration. It reaches out into the state legislative assemblies, state government, and state administrations. It is an expanding political culture. And although it is permeated with traditional elements, it is not wholly traditional for it has many modern components. The second political culture predominates in New Delhi. It can be found among India's planners, many of the national political leadership, and in the senior administrative cadre...It trickless off as one moves into state capitals, though it can be found there too, and almost disappears as one looks into rural areas of municipal government...The first can be characterezed as an elite mass political culture, and the second as an elite political culture. (Weiner 1967:114)

The data in this study do not show a significant difference between state and national political and industrial cultures (Table X and XV). There is no doubt that "with each election", there has been a decline in the number of members of parliament who command English and in their average level of education". (Hardgrave 1980:114) While command of the English language is not a 'prerequisite' of modern political culture, the level of education is and a low level could have a serious dysfunctional impact on the direction of modernization and social change and the nature of political and industrial cultures. In this context Kothari's (1970:282) distinction between earlier 'modernist' and more recent 'modernizers' is noteworthy. The earlier 'modernists' were predominantly urban, urbane, Brahmanic, and more ideological. The recent 'modernizers' are rural, peasant proprietors, modest merchants, more pragmatic, and closer to people. The direction of Indian politics is moving toward the more pragmatic politics of Mrs. Indira Gandhi rather than the ideological Nehru-style politics.

Table XV

Elite Profile of Industrial Culture and Level of Modernity

Level of Modernity	Industrial India	Culture U.P.
High	High	High
Moderate	Moderate	Moderate
Low	Low	Low

In a country like India where the difference between prosperity and poverty hangs on a monsoon, the politics of performance is crucial to political stability and change. Ideology provides direction. Without performance it is meaningless. Pragmatic-ideological politics provides "rotee, kapra, aur makaan" (bread, clothing, and housing). It does not have to be parochial or traditional. Modernity and pragmatism are inseparable. For thirty-four years democracy has survived, and a consensus has emerged on the fundamental rules of the game. Most of the present leaders in national politics have spent considerable time in state politics. (Singh and Vajpeyi 1973) The gap between the two political cultures is decreasing as evidenced by the above data.

In conclusion, the emerging political culture among Indian elites is that of integration, commitment to a democratic system, egalitarian society, socialism, commitment to statism, industrialization and technologicalization. There exists a consensus among elites about fundamental issues and the rules of the game. It is due to this integrative value system that "...political elite, operating through an institutionalized apparatus of regional linkages and having a strong propensity to subordinate internal disagreements to a preference for consensus, has been a key variable in stabilizing India through political change since independence". (Headrick 1973:565) It is because of such orientations that India has been able to develop a relatively high degree of consensus in the crucial areas of policy-making such as economic planning, democratic system, egalitarian society, and foreign policy. The Indian elites, given such a framework, have been able to commit themselves to a developmental ideology and operate as functional elites. Normative consensus is very fragile and much has yet to be done. These values have to be internalized and transferred to the masses. Only then will the dreams of nation-building, political development, and modernization be complete. The data reported in this study show that a good start has been made. The seeds planted during the nationalist movement and immediately after independence in an effort to create a modern democratic

India on the basis of a traditional value system yet without sacrificing its cultural heritage are beginning to grow. At least that's the hope and direction to which the present study points.

NOTES

1   "Technology may be defined as the systematic application of collective human rationality to the solution of problems by asserting control over nature and over human processes of all kinds". Goulet, Denis, 1977 '*The Uncertain Promise*', Washington, D.C., Overseas Development Council; p. 6.
2   Almond and Powell (1966) in their discussion of political culture point out three directions:
    1. Substantive content consists of 'system' culture, 'process' culture, and 'policy' culture. The 'system' culture of a nation will include the distribution of attitudes toward the national community, the regime, and the authorities, the sense of national identity, attitude toward the legitimacy of the regime and the various institutions, attitude toward the legitimacy and effectiveness of the incumbents of the various political roles. The 'process' culture of a nation will consist of attitudes toward the self in politics, attitudes toward other political actors—the feelings of trust, cooperation, competence, and hostility. The 'policy' culture will include the distribution of preferences regarding the outputs and outcomes of politics, and the ordering among different groupings in the population of values related to liberty, security, welfare, change, and modernization. Orientations and attitudes toward these 'systems', 'process', and 'policy' objectives could be *Cognitive*—beliefs, information and analysis; *Affective*—feelings of attachment, aversion or indifference; *Evaluative*—moral judgments.
    2. The systematic relations among the components.
    3. Varieties of orientations and attitudes.
A discussion of the political culture has to address itself to all three of these components.

REFERENCES

AIKEN, Michael, and MOTT, Paul
    1970   *The Structure of Community Power*, New York: Random House.
ALMOND, Gabriel and POWELL, Bingham
    1966   *Comparative Politics: A Developmental Approach*, Boston: Little Brown and Company.
BONJEAN, Charles M., Terry N. CLARK and Robert L. LINEBERRY
    1971   *Community Parties: A Behavioral Approach*, New York: Free Press.
BURNHAM, James
    1942   *The Managerial Revolution*, London: Putnam.
CARROL, Lewis
    1965   *Alice Through The Looking Glass*, New York: The Macmillan Company.
CLARK, Terry N.
    1968   *Community Structure and Decision-Making: Comparative Analysis*, San Francisco: Chandler Publishing Company.
CLARKE, Arthur C.
    1964   *Profiles of the Future*, New York: Bantam. (Clarke imagined Cyborgs as biological forms that incorporate with computers and other technical devices to expand man's natural powers).
DRUCKER, Peter
    1957   *Landmarks of Tomorrow*, New York: Harper and Row.
ELLUL, Jacques
    1964   *The Technological Society*, New York: Knopf.

FERKISS, Victor
    1969   *Technological Man: The Myth and the Reality*, New York: George Braziller.
FLERON, Fred
    1969   "Cooperation as a Mechanism of Adaptation to Change: The Soviet Political
            Leadership System", *Polity II*, Winter.
GOLDMAN, R. D., R. B. PLATT and R. B. KAPLAN
    1973   "Dimensions of Attitudes Toward Technology", *Journal of Applied Psychology*, 57.
GOULET, Denis
    1977   *The Uncertain Promise*, Washington, D.C.: Overseas Development Council.
GUNNEL, John C.
    1970   "Development, Social Change, and Time", in Waldo Dwight (ed.), *Temporal
            Dimensions of Development Administration*, North Carolina, Duke University Press.
HARDGRAVE, Robert
    1980   *India, Government and Politics in a Developing Nation*, New York: Hartcourt Brace
            Javanovich, Inc.
HEADRICK, Thomas E.
    1973   "Crisis and Continuity: India in the Mid-1960's", in Gabriel Almond, et al, *Crisis
            and Change, Historical Studies of Political Development*, Boston: Little Brown and Com-
            pany.
HUSSAIN, A. F. A.
    1956   *Human and Social Impact of Technological Change in Pakistan*, Dacca: Oxford University
            Press.
India
    1980   New Delhi: Publications Division. (46.4% of the total investment during the First
            Five Year Plan (1951-1956) climbed to 66% by the Fifth Five Year Plan.
JACOB, Philip *et al.*
    1971   *Values and Active Community: A Cross-national Study of Local Leadership*, New York: Free
            Press.
JEQUIER, Nicholas (ed.)
    1976   *Appropriate Technology: Problems and Promises*, Paris: OECD.
KAHN, Herman, and Anthony WEINER
    1967   *The Year 2000*, New York: The Macmillan Company.
KOTHARI, Rajni
    1970   *Politics in India*, Boston: Little Brown and Company.
LAPORTE, T. R., and D. METLAY
    1975   "Public Attitudes Toward Present and Future Technologies: Satisfactions and Ap-
            prehensions", *Social Studies of Science.*
LEE, Hahn-Been
    1970   "Developmentalist in Time Development Entrepreneurs, and Leadership in
            Developing Countries", in Waldo (ed.). *op. cit.*
LERNER, Daniel
    1968   *The Passing of Traditional Society*, New York: Free Press.
LINTON, Ralph
    1952   "Cultural and Personality Factors Affecting Economic Growth", in Bert F.
            Holeditz (ed.), *The Progress of Underdeveloped Areas*, Chicago: University of Chicago
            Press.
MARTIN, P. W.
    1955   *Experiment in Depth: A Study of the Work of Jung, Eliot, and Toynbee*, London: Routledge
            and Kegal Paul.
McHALE, John
    1969   *The Future of the Future*, New York: Braziller.
MEDHORA, Pheroze B.
    1973   "Managerial Reforms in India's Public Sector", *South Asian Review*, 7, I, October.
MOSCA, Gaetano
    1939   *The Ruling Class*, edited and revised by Arthur Livingstone, translated by Hannah D.
            Kahn, New York: McGraw-Hill.

MUKHERJEE, Ramkrishna
1977 *Scientific Technological Revolution: Social Aspects*, California: Sage Publications.
MULLER, Herbert
1970 *Children of Frankenstein: A Primer on Modern Technology and Human Values*, Bloomington: Indiana University Press.
NADEL, S. F.
1956 "The Concept of Social Elites", *International Social Science Bulletin*, 8.
PARKIN, Frank
1971 *Class Inequality and Political Order: Social Stratification in Capitalist and Communist Societies*", London: MacGibbon and Kee.
PARSONS, Talcott
1951 The *Social System*, Glencoe, Illinois: The Free Press.
POLYANI, Karl
1957 *The Great Transformation: The Political and Economic Origins of Our Times*, Boston: Beacon Press.
RAMESH, Jairam
1981 "Technology '80", *Seminar*, January.
Resolutions on Economic Policy and Program
1955 1924-54, New Delhi, All India Congress Committee.
SCHWARTZ, Eugene. S.
1971 *Overkill: The Decline of Technology in Modern Civilization*, New York: Quadrangle.
SINGH, Baljit, and VAJPEYI, Dhirendra
1973 *Political Stability in Indian States: A Satistical Analysis 1947-1964*, East Lansing, Michigan State University: Asian Studies Center.
STANLEY, Manfred
1978 *The Technological Conscience: Survival and Dignity in an Age of Expertise*, New York: Free Press.
TAVISS, I.
1972 "A Survey of Popular Attitudes Toward Technology", *Technology and Culture.*
THEORDORSEN, George A.
1953 "Acceptance of Industrialization and Its Attendant Consquences for Social Patterns of Non-Western Societies", *American Sociological Review*, 18, October.
VAJPEYI, Dhirendra
1979 *Social Change and Modernization in India*, Delhi: Manohar.
VONNEGUT, Jr., Kurt
1967 *Player Piano*, New York: Holt, Rinehart, and Winston.
WEINER, Myron
1967 *State Politics in India*, Princeton, New Jersey: Princeton University Press.
WITHEY, S.
1959 "Public Opinion About Science and Scientists", *Public Opinion Quarterly.*
WRIGHT, A. T.
1942 *Islandia*, New York: Rinehart.

Technocrats and the Generalist Mystique
Physicians, Engineers, and the Administrative System of Pakistan

CHARLES H. KENNEDY

Bowdoin College Brunswick, U.S.A.

DURING THE SUMMER of 1982 junior staff physicians participated in work slowdowns at various hospitals throughout Pakistan. Their demands—to upgrade the status and the terms and conditions of employment for government physicians—were reminiscent of demands voiced most stridently by engineers and seconded by physicians thirteen years earlier during the so-called "Disturbances of 1968-9". Clearly, these two events were not isolated incidents, nor were their similarities coincidental; rather, they were a product of the long-simmering grievances of technocrats[1] with the administrative system of Pakistan. This paper attempts to explain the causes of these grievances, to trace their expression, and to describe the Government's response to the resultant demands. To approach this task the paper serially addresses four relevant questions: (1) Why are the technocrats upset? (2) What did the technocrats want in 1968-9? (3) What did the technocrats get as a consequence of the reforms of 1973? And, (4) What do the technocrats still want in 1982?

I. Why are the Technocrats Upset? Characteristics and Outcomes of the Administrative System of Pakistan

A discussion of the role or status of technocrats in Pakistan is inextricably linked with the norms and structures of the bureaucracy of which such technocrats are a part. Therefore, a fruitful point of departure for this paper is a discussion of the dominant characteristics of the administrative system of Pakistan. In broad strokes there are three such characteristics: (a) The secretariat system of bureaucratic authority, (b) the systemic preference for generalists, and (c) the cadre system of organization. We will look at these in turn.

(a) *The Secretariat System of Bureaucratic Authority*

Under the terms of the Constitution of 1972, the Government of Pakistan has a ministerial form of organization. At last count (1982) there were nineteen ministries, each of which contains one or more administrative "divisions". Typically each division is composed of a central secretariat, the appropriate attached departments, and the "autonomous" and/or "semi-autonomous" organizations affiliated with the division. For example, the Establishment Division, part of the ministry-level Cabinet Secretariat, is composed of a central secretariat in Islamabad, several attached departments, the most prominent of which are the Federal Service Tribunal and the All-Pakistan Administrative Research Centre, and several autonomous bodies including the Pakistan Administrative Staff College and the Civil Services Academy. There is no ironclad rule which defines the relationship between attached departments or autonomous organizations and their respective central secretariat. For the most part, however, autonomous organizations are more independent of their parent secretariat than attached departments. Usually directors of the former are directly responsible to the Secretary of the division, while heads of attached departments are usually responsible to secretariat officers subordinate to the Secretary. Also, autonomous organizations are usually larger than attached departments. However, in practice one finds numerous exceptions to both of these rules.

The combined strength of attached departments and autonomous organizations dwarf the respective sizes of the central secretariats. The latest available data indicates that a total of 13,062 public servants worked in the parent organizations of the federal secretariat in 1980, while 108,091 worked in analogous attached departments [GOP, O + M Division: 1981: 27-56] and as many as 185,841 (1975) worked in autonomous or semi-autonomous organizations. [GOP, O + M Wing:1975] Moreover, compared to attached departments and autonomous or semi-autonomous organizations, the central secretariat employs proportionately more officer-level employees. In 1980, 22 percent of the employees of the central secretariat held posts at National Pay Scale (NPS) Grade 17 or above, while comparable percentages for attached departments were 3 percent and for autonomous organizations (1975) 9 percent. [GOP, O + M Division:1981; GOP, O + M Wing:1975]

As this structure of organization indicates, the administrative system of Pakistan firmly adheres to the conceptual dichotomy between staff and line officers. Ideally, staff officers, (secretariat officers), provide the policy direction for programs, assess the effectiveness or ineffectiveness of these programs, modify the scope of given programs, take ultimately the final responsibility for personnel decisions and training of officers, serve as the liaison between administrative institutions within the bureaucracy, and act as the conduit through which political control is exercised. Line officers, (officers in attached departments and autonomous organizations), on the other hand, execute the programs which the staff officers introduce. Or as bureaucrats in Pakistan are likely to state: "Staff officers are the head and line officers are the body".

In practice, there is a great deal of variation in the amount of control secretariat officers actually exercise over attached departments and autonomous or semi-autonomous organizations. The primary determinants of the level of such control are the level of technical expertise required to deal with any relevant policy, and the personalities and ambitions of the individual officers concerned. Nevertheless, adherence to this dichotomy has two important implications for the career patterns of bureaucrats. First, line officers typically are placed lower in the rank hierarchy of the service structure than secretariat officers holding comparable posts. That is, the typical senior-level line officer, a head of a department, usually holds a post with the equivalent rank of Deputy Secretary—NPS 19. A comparable officer in the secretariat typically will hold a post in the rank of Joint Secretary—NPS 20. Therefore, the promotional prospects of secretariat officers are more sanguine than such prospects for line officers. Second, the career patterns of secretariat officers are open to considerable diversity and inter-institutional mobility. Indeed, the rule of thumb in assigning officers to secretariat postings is to keep officers in a given assignment for at least eighteen months but for no longer than three years. Conversely, line officer's careers are limited, except in extraordinary circumstances, to assignment within their parent line department. The combination of these factors make assignment to secretariat postings much more attractive to prospective officers of the bureaucracy of Pakistan. Not only are the prospects for promotion and the attendant perquisites related to such promotion better for secretariat officers, but the likelihood of meaningful and varied employment is also comparatively greater as well.

(b) *The Systemic Preference for Generalists*

Both a cause and a consequence of the secretariat system of authority is the long-standing principle of the preference for the selection of generalist administrators to fill secretariat posts. As noted above, heads of departments, who for the most part are technocrats, are responsible to secretariat officers who, in contrast, predominantly possess generalist backgrounds.

More fundamental, however, is the system of recruitment employed to select officers for the bureaucracy. Pakistan's system of recruitment is biased to favor generalists and it succeeds in implementing this bias. Of course, such bias has a long institutional history in South Asia and can be traced back at least as far as Thomas Babington Macaulay's oft-quoted defense of direct competition for entry to the Covenanted Civil Services:

> It is said I know that examination in Latin, in Greek and in Mathematics are no tests of what men will prove to be in life. I am perfectly aware that they are not infallible tests; but that they are tests I confidently maintain. Look at any walk of life—the House—at the other House—at the Bar—at the Bench—at the Church—and see whether it not be true that those who attain high distinction in the world are generally men who are distinguished in their academic career. [Great Britain, Parliament:1853:Cols. 750-3]

Macaulay's side won the day in the debate before the House of Commons, and one year later in 1854, he was made President of a Committee entrusted with the task of implementing the Government of India Act of 1853. Under the direction of Macaulay, the Committee recommended that the competitive examination should be designed to test the general education of candidates, where "general education" was defined in terms of a traditional liberal arts program at an Oxbridge-style university. Consequently, the syllabus of the proposed exam included general science, mathematics, European literature, and modern and classical languages, with the inevitable mid-nineteenth century reliance on Greek and Latin. [Great Britain, Parliament:1854:25] Only two subjects tested in the competitive examinations had direct non-European origins—Sanskrit and Arabic. It was taken for granted that this examination was to be conducted only in English and was to be administered exclusively in Britain. Finally, the Committee restricted entry to service to only those candidates who fell within the age range 18 to 23. [Great Britain, Parliament: 1854:27-9] This, of course, reinforced the already strong presumption that candidates to service would usually be drawn from the pool of new graduates of British universities.

Though there have been modifications from time to time, the adoption of these recommendations established the basic structure of the competitive examination. In other words, the recommendations of the Macaulay Committee established that the competitive examination should be a test of general education, that the goal of the selection process was to recruit candidates who possessed academic promise, that the examination should primarily test knowledge concerning topics of European culture, and that the examination should be conducted in English. None of these latter recommendations was ever seriously challenged prior to Partition, and indeed they remain largely valid in Pakistan today.

To substantiate this latter contention one has only to examine the selection process for direct recruits as it functions in 1982. Would be members of the Central Superior Services (Federal Unified Grade)[2] must first possess the equivalent of a Second Division Bachelor's degree from a recognized Pakistani or foreign institution and/or an advanced degree (A.M., etc.) of any Division. They also, with certain exceptions, must be between the ages of 21 to 25.[3] If an individual meets these requirements he may then participate in the combined CSS Examination[4] held annually throughout Pakistan, and administered by the Federal Public Service Commission. Typically, a candidate devotes several months subsequent to graduation in preparation for the exam. It is also not uncommon for individual candidates to appear more than once for the exam in order to improve their relative standing in the competition.

The CSS Examination itself is composed of four parts: a written examination, the "viva voce", psychological testing, and a medical examination. The written examination carries a total of 1100 marks divided between compulsory and optional subjects. Compulsory subjects, which carry a total of 500 marks, are English essay, English precis and composition, everyday science, current affairs and Pakistan affairs.[5] Each of these examinations is designed to take three hours to complete and carries equivalent weighting, (100 marks). The purpose of this section of the exam is designed to test each candidate's facility in English, as well as his/her general knowledge of the socio-political environment. Whether the CSS Examination is an adequate measure of these attitudes is debatable. The exam is vulnerable to the charges that it may overstress the importance of English, [Husain:1979] that it may require the recall of largely irrelevant or unimportant detail, and/or that the exam relies too heavily on Western cultural traditions.[6] The optional section of the written portion of the CSS Exam, on the other hand, is designed to test a candidate's knowledge of self selected academic disciplines. With certain restrictions in regard to combinations of subjects, candidates choose the optional subjects to total 600 marks, (optional subjects carry varied weightings), from 50-odd available subjects covering the range of standard university offerings.[7]

The "viva voce" is an interview before members of the Federal Public Service Commission, members of the Establishment Division, and other government officials. Here, the candidate's composure, temperament, etc. are tested. This exercise carries 300 marks. The psychological and medical tests carry no marks, but adverse findings on either of these evaluations may veto an otherwise acceptable candidate's appointment.

Subsequent to the completion of these four parts of the examination, each individual's score is totalled and subject to the number of vacancies to service, and to regional quota considerations [Kennedy:1982(1); Kennedy:1982(2)] candidates are declared successful or unsuccessful, and if successful are assigned to an occupational group, and are admitted to the Civil Services Academy for combined pre-service training.[8]

Given the generalist bias of the CSS Examination both in regard to the content of its evaluation and in regard to its administration, it is not surprising that successful recruits to the CSS Examination also are predominantly generalists. Table One describes the educational backgrounds of successful recruits for the years 1970-1976. A perusal of this Table reveals that the profile of an archetypical successful recruit has changed little during the six years described by the data.[9] Typically, such recruits possess an M.A. in behavioral sciences, (most likely political science or economics), or the arts, (most likely English or English literature). Relatively few candidates have a background in the sciences and of these the great majority, (90% in 1976), do not possess an advanced degree in science. The inescapable conclusion is that direct recruitment through the CSS Exam serves to select generalists for induction into the service.

Obviously then, technocrats must enter the bureaucracy through mechanisms other than the CSS Examination. Until 1976 engineers, unlike other professionals, were inducted into federal service positions through the process of a separate direct competitive examination conducted by the FPSC. This examination tested both general knowledge and specific technical expertise. [GOP, Federal Public Service Commission:1976] The last such examination was held in 1976 and upon the recommendation of the FPSC [GOP, Federal Public Service Commission:1978:14-5] it was replaced by a system which subjects qualified engineers to an interview by the FPSC for specific posts. The recruitment of physicians, who for the most part enter health departments under the authority of relevant provicial governments, has never fallen under the purview of the FPSC. The selection of members of other technical professions qua profession has also never been subject to systematic federal recruitment.

Given this state of affairs, the great bulk of technocrats enter the bureaucracy through the process of answering advertisements announcing

Table 1

Educational Background, Successful Direct Recruits to the
Federal Bureaucracy of Pakistan, 1970-1976

I.	Degree Held	1970^a	1971	1972	1973	1974	1976
PhD	-	-	-	1(1)	2(1)	-	
	Double MA	-	9(3)	9(4)	10(5)	3(1)	3(2)
	MA and Law	19(2)	24(7)	20(10)	30(14)	26(12)	13(9)
	MA	109(67)	233(64)	138(66)	120(57)	129(58)	94(63)
	BA and Law	1(1)	22(6)	28(13)	16(8)	30(14)	16(11)
	BA	34(21)	78(21)	16(8)	35(17)	33(17)	23(15)
	Missing	203	0	50	0	0	2

II.	Academic Speciality	1970^a	1971	1972	1973	1974	1976
	Arts:	78(22)	64(31)	68(32)	80(36)	48(32)	
	English	48	45	45	33	23	
	English Literature	2	3	9	24	12	
	History	11	10	8	10	3	
	Other	17	6	6 13	10		
	Behavoral Sciences:	201(58)	113(54)	106(50)	113(51)	72(48)	
	Political Science	82	41	47	36	31	
	Economics	93	55	44	63	32	
	Public Administration	4	7	4	4	4	
	Business	4	4	8	5	2	
	Other	18	6	3	5	3	
	Science:	71(20)	32(15)	38(18)	29(13)	30(20)	
	Physics	22	5	9	3	6	
	Chemistry	7	5	5	7	9	
	Math	7	3	2	5	1	
	Life Science	10	6	6	3	6	
	Engineering	12	6	6	5	5	
	Other	13	52	0	1	20	

(Figures in parentheses are adjusted frequencies, deleting missing data, within batch).

[a]Available information for the 1970 batch included only successful candidates after the results of the "First Allocation" to service. This explains the relatively high proportion of missing data.

Source: Compiled by author from biodata of probationers.

specific vacancies in relevant departments. As a consequence most engineers find employment with autonomous corporations; most physicians with provincial health departments. As we will see below, neither of these categories confers "civil servant" status on its members.

The system of pre-service training of direct recruits does little to ameliorate the consequences of this generalist bias. Indeed, in some regards, it reinforces such tendencies. The Civil Services Academy, the main locus of such pre-service training, attempts to accomplish several ambitious tasks:

> "(a) To prepare the probationers for induction into the public service, (b) to acquaint them with the ideology of Pakistan, (c) to acquiant them with the environment of public administration in Pakistan, (d) to acquaint them with modern concepts and techniques of administration and management, (e) to create an awareness of the need for economic and social development and the ability to play an efficient role in the process, (f) to inculcate a feeling of equality and fraternity among public servants, (g) to develop their sense of public duty and to mould them into efficient, hardworking, and devoted public servants. [GOP, Civil Services Academy:1980]

Like its predecessor the CSA fulfills some of these tasks better than others. Clearly, its strength lies in the process of socialization of officers for the bureaucracy, and given limited resources and competencies, not in training technically-efficient decision makers. [Kennedy:1979:223-32]

Finally, after the officer assumes regular posting in the field, this generalist bias is further reinforced by the organizational environment to which he is subject. First, transfers are frequent and as a consequence the officer usually cannot gain substantive expertise in any given field of administration. Second, there is no personal incentive for officers to work at gaining such expertise. Indeed within bureaucratic circles there are strong group pressures to not dirty one's hands in the day-to-day activities of line departments. Finally, given the organizational relationship between secretariat officers and line officers, there is little institutional incentive to establish specialties. Heads of departments are responsible for the field operations; secretariat officers are merely responsible for formulating what such field officers should do. The characteristics required for this latter task are tact and the capacity to compromise. In essence, secretariat officers are brokers between political authority and operations in the field.

(c) *The Cadre System of Organization*

Undergirding and interacting with the two preceding conditions is the prevalent pattern of the compartmentalization of bureaucrats into semi-functional occupational groupings, collectively referred to as "services", "cadres", or "groups". All recruits upon the successful completion of the CSS Examination are assigned a position in an occupational group.[10] In 1982, there were eleven such groups: Accounts Group, Commerce and Trade Group, Customs and Excise Group, District Management Group, Foreign Affairs Group, Income Tax Group, Information Group, Military Lands and Cantonment Group, Police Group, Postal Group, and Railways Group.[11] Most of these groups have a long institutional history and some of them can trace their origins to the late-nineteenth century. [Kennedy:1979:42-68]

Though the careers of officers once assigned to groups typically falls loosely within the range covered by the functional specialty implied in group nomenclature, the original assignment to occupational groups is not directly based on the functional specialties of individual recruits. Rather such assignment is the consequence of the confluence of three factors: (1) Score/ranking on the CSS Examination, (2) domicile of candidate (regional quota), and (3) the recruit's individual preference. That is, candidates are assigned to occupational groups on the basis of their individual preference prioritized by the order of their ranking on the CSS Examination for their category of domicile. As a consequence, no functional specialization is presupposed of officers assigned to particular occupational groups. Indeed some occupational groups rely on separate pre-service training to inculcate such specialization.

In the main, once an individual is assigned to a group he remains a member of that cadre throughout his career, and his promotional prospects, job type, duties, prestige, and so forth are determined to a great extent by association with the cadre. Typically, cadres are "reserved" and the members normally fill certain posts in the secretariat. For instance, the position of Postal Inspector is usually filled by a member of the Postal Group, Commissioner by a member of the District Management Group, Collector of Taxes by a member of the Income Tax Group, and so forth. To gain such a post then, an individual must be a member of the relevant cadre and have sufficient cadre-wise seniority to compete with other aspirants. That is, individual mobility through the lens of the cadre system is analogous to Srivanas' concept of caste mobility. [Srinivas:1967] If one's caste, (occupational cadre), is upwardly mobile, one's individual career prospects are bright and vice versa.

Officers with federal cadre affiliation dominate policy-making positions in the central secretariat. For instance in 1982, of the 39 regular Secretary appointments, NPS 22 in the Secretariat Group,[12] 35 were members of a federal occupational cadre. [GOP, Establishment Division:1982]

Also of great significance are the profound differences in the status and prestige which accrue to membership in particular cadres. At the top of the hierarchy, prior to 1973, was the Civil Service of Pakistan, (CSP).[13] High-ranking posts were "reserved" for members of this cadre throughout the central secretariat and in district administration. Similarly, members of this cadre were awarded higher scales of pay than were members of other cadres. Further, promotional prospects, training facilities, housing allowances, responsibilities/duties, etc. were designed to favor CSP officers. Coupled with these organizational distinctions were distinctions in the social elements of prestige. For instance, the CSP was perceived to be the elite of the service structure and in social contexts its members were accorded levels of status comparable to judicial or highly-placed political officials. Membership in the CSP Association, (the cadre's interest group), conferred enormous benefits. There was almost a familial relationship between members of the CSP, reinforced by professional interaction, but nurtured primarily by "old school ties", mutual attendance at the CSP Academy.

Though such advantages have been toned down since the administrative reforms of 1973, members of the elite cadres still dominate top positions in the secretariat, as evidenced by the fact that 29 of the 39 regular Secretary positions in the Secretariat Group are still held (1982) by former CSP officers. Beneath these "Brahmins" is a broad spectrum of "Kshatriyas" whose most-favored sects include the Foreign Affairs Group, and the Customs and Excise Group. Clearly subordinate are various less-favored sects of the Federal Unified Grades such as the Postal Group, or the now defunct Office Management Group. However, membership in a federal occupational group, regardless of affiliation, confers "twice-born" status on its members. Officers without such cadre affiliation are the "untouchables" of the administrative system.

One consequence of the generalist bias of the selection process for direct recruits, (described above), is that technically-trained individuals, typically not selected by the process of direct recruitment, are also perforce not subject to the sanguine career prospects which come with federal cadre affiliation. The strategy employed by professional groups, particularly engineers and physicians, has been to form or to attempt to form their own cadres. Engineers became members of the Central Engineering Service and Telegraph and Telephone Service while physicians became members of provincial services—such as the West Pakistan Health Service. [Kennedy:1979:57-60] However, such cadre affiliation was banned after the reforms of 1973, and even in their heyday such cadres were but a pale reflection of federal cadres.

Therefore, in sum, the characteristics of Pakistan's administrative system have been and remain stacked in favor of generalists and against technocrats. Staff officers, (primarily, generalists), are favored over line officers, (primarily, technocrats), in terms of career prospects, and administrative authority. Direct recruitment, the main avenue to staff appointments, is dominated by a generalist bias which results in the filling of most entry-level positions with promising "all-rounders". And, finally, federal cadre affiliation, the main determinant of individual mobility within the system, is functionally, denied to bureaucrats who enter the system through non-direct means. Given these characteristics, there is little wonder why the technocrats were and have remained dissatisfied with the bureaucratic system of Pakistan. We will now turn our attention to an analysis of the form such dissatisfaction has taken.

II. What the Technocrats Wanted: Physician and Engineering Demands and the Disturbances of 1968-9

As we have demonstrated above, technocrats have had long-standing grievances with the bureaucratic system of Pakistan. However, these grievances did not translate into political action until late 1968 and early 1969 when physicians and engineers became the vanguard of intra-bureaucratic dissent during the Disturbances. As several scholars have argued [Muneer:1978; Sayeed:1979; Kennedy:1982(3); Heeger:1977; Burki:1972] the late '60's was a particularly propitious time for the venting of political steam. President Ayub's decade-long formula of civil-military authoritarianism was under service attack from several directions and change seemed imminent.

Physicians were among the first to stage an assault from within the bureaucracy itself. As early as November 11, [*Pakistan Times*, November 12, 1968] the Executive Committee of the West Pakistan Health Service Association demanded Class I status, (officer-level status, the same as accorded CSS recruits), for new recruits to their service. They also pushed for several other policies which would have had the collective effect of improving the terms and conditions of service for physicians within the bureaucracy. These demands spread rapidly and found ready acceptance among students and doctors attached to medical colleges. Indeed by January 11, medical personnel at Liaquat Medical Hospital, Peshawar and Nishtar Medical Hospital, Multan had organized protest marches. [*Pakistan Times*: January 12, 1969] Four days later 200 junior doctors in Karachi took up the cause and staged a token strike. [*Pakistan Times*: January 16, 1969] Finally, 24-hour provincial strikes organized by the newly-formed "Central Medical Body" were staged on January 18 [*Pakistan Times*: Jan. 19, 1969] and February 14. [*PT*: Feb. 15, 1969]

The Government's response to such demands was lukewarm at best. Muneer goes so far as to say that the Government even made veiled threats to fire recalcitrant medical personnel and replace them with RCD doctors. [Muneer:1978:29] In any case, the Government's unresponsiveness to the demands fueled even more radical responses by medical personnel. On March 5, the CMB declared a "general strike for an indefinite period". [*PT*:March 6, 1969] This got the attention of the Government and on March 9 they responded by accepting the most important of the physician's demands, i.e., to accord Class I status to new recruits of the West Pakistan Health Services. [*PT*:March 10, 1969] Upon receipt of this concession the strike ended.

While the demands of physicians remained relatively limited, and, once accepted, easily addressed by the Government, the demands of engineers were much more fundamental to the operation of the bureaucratic system as a whole. In other words, the engineers became more directly embroiled in the issue of specialist vs. generalist. At first, however, the engineers followed the lead of the medical personnel. In December 1968 the "Lahore Engineering Students" later seconded by the "Engineering Students Welfare Association" and the "Student Action Committee of the West Pakistan University of Engineering and Technology" demanded that new engineering recruits, (B.S. Eng.), be uniformly accorded Class I status. [Muneer:1978:30] And, as in the case of medical personnel, student engineers took to the streets in January 1969 to press their demands. But as it became increasingly clear that the Government had decided to turn a deaf ear to such demands, the ad hoc "Engineers Action Committee" decided to change its strategy by addressing system-wide issues. On February 13 some 2000 senior engineers joined by hundreds of engineering students marched in Lahore. Among their more radical demands were the implementation of the "Cornelius Report", a document which had recommended substantial administrative reforms favorable to technocrats, [GOP, Cabinet Secretariat:1969] the abolishment of the CSP, and the establishment of a system that would reserve technical posts for engineers. [PT:Feb. 14, 1969] Following a successful three day strike by the Telegraph Engineer's Association on March 11-14, [PT:March 15, 1969] a prospective and indefinite general strike of engineers in support of this widescale reform was only forestalled by the imposition of Martial Law.

The resignation of President Ayub on March 25 and the imposition of Martial Law under General Yahya Khan led to the placing of the generalist-specialist issue squarely on the policy agenda. First, the actions of the physicians, engineers, and of other professional groups during the Disturbances had served to politicize the grievances of the technocrats. Second, the public's perception of the orthodox bureaucracy, and particularly of its elite cadres, had undergone a not-so-subtle transformation. During the Disturbances the alleged deficiencies of the bureaucracy—corruption, malfeasance, laziness, mediocrity, aloofness—were publicized in spectacular ways through the streets of Pakistan. Indeed, provincial secretariats were attacked twice by angry mobs incited by charges that the bureaucracy was corrupt. Of course, the CSP as the symbol of the bureaucratic establishment, had come under the most scathing criticism, both from disaffected service associations, and from opposition politicians who saw the cadre as a bulwark of President Ayub's power. [Kennedy:1982(3):47-51]

General Yahya responded with two policies: (1) the purge of allegedly corrupt officials, and (2) the establishment of a Services Reorganisation Committee to contemplate reform. On December 2, 1969, Yahya under the terms of Martial Law no. 58, removed 303 Class I officers from service. Many of the officers were highly-placed—38 of them were members of the CSP and a total of 78 were from the Central Superior Services. [Kennedy:1982(3):50] The establishment of the Services Reorganisation Committee in November under the chairmanship of Justice Cornelius, provides evidence that the Government had chosen to meet the criticisms of the bureaucracy by reforming its structure. From the terms of reference of the Committee:

> Among the causes of public resentment, which led to country-wide demonstrations during the period preceding Martial Law on March 25, 1969, the resentment against the structure of administration of the country figures prominently. People in all walks of life including a majority of those in government services condemned this structure on the grounds that
> - it was a relic of the colonial past in which the relationship between the government functionaries and the people was that of ruler and ruled
> - it had during the last 22 years proved to be unsuited to the needs and aspirations of a free and sovereign people
> - it had continued to sustain and even to strengthen a ruling elite within the service cadres, which had sacrificed administrative neutrality for political partisanship
> - it had helped to promote corruption, inefficiency, and selfishness. [GOP:1971:v]

Once formed the Services Reorganisation Committee served as a forum to express the demands of service associations for reform of the bureaucracy. Indeed, the SRC took an active role by soliciting the opinions of a wide range of groups and individuals[14] representing virtually every relevant interest in bureaucratic reform. Prominent among such participants were interest groups representing physicians and engineers. Our analysis which follows is derived from a careful reading of the relevant documents submitted to the Committee. In particular we examined the service petitions of fifteen engineering associations[15] and four physician's associations.[16] Without doing too much injustice to the welter of arguments found in these petitions, nor to the sometimes wide differences in the degree of expression of such arguments, one can boil down the mixture into a fairly coherent technocratic critique of the bureaucratic system, and into a package of recommendations which flow from that critique. We will deal with these in turn.

The Technocratic Critique of the Bureaucratic System

Running through the physician and engineering service association demands are four interrelated themes. The first theme is that Pakistan's bureaucratic system and particularly its reliance upon generalist administration is a product of the much-maligned colonial legacy. As a consequence, Pakistan's bureaucratic system is portrayed as profoundly undemocratic and crafted more to serve the needs of a colonial master than a sovereign people. The following description of the bureaucracy is not atypical: "several thousand public servants of which a few hundred were the elite assumed the position of rulers of the teeming millions". [EPWAPDA:1970:§5] Attributed to this legacy are several ills: the overbearing attitude of public servants to the public, [EPWAPDA: 1970: § 6] the lack of public accountability of bureaucrats, [EPWAPDA: 1970: § 7,19] economic and political underdevelopment, [CES: 1970: § 2-3] inherent class distinctions within the bureaucracy which undermine "cooperation, coordination, and team spirit", [EPWAPDA: 1970: § 13] lack of professionalism, [PMS: 1970: § 7-13] and, of course, the generalist bias itself. [EPESA: 1970: § 10-12]

The second theme is that generalist officers are inefficient at best, and often corrupt. This is attributed partially to the structural dimensions of the bureaucratic system, structures which "date back to the East India Company" and which place undue authority and hence temptation in the hands of senior public officials. [EPWAPDA:1970:§11] But it is also attributed to the selection process of individuals to fill such posts of authority, a process which selects an ambitious though a "second-rate residue" of talent. [EPESA:1970:§8-9]

Closely related to the foregoing is a third theme which argues that generalist officers are incompetent or at least not as deserving as technocrats for senior administrative postings. This theme is reiterated frequently in the service demands and the following quotations present the substance of the argument:

The best students in Primary Schools grasp well science and mathematics. After Matriculation, first class students continue with science with medicine or non-medical subjects and the best lot getting through Intermediate Examination goes to engineering, medicine, pure sciences, defence services, etc., the top talent eventually becoming professionals in their field of specialisation. Some of the residue students who cannot make their headway in Commerce, Industry and other services elsewhere take part in the CSP Examination.

The situation in regard to the Provincial Civil Services is worse...

Now recruitment in these services is being made through Public Service Commissions. But the people who compete for these services are the residue left after repeated filtrations. First filtration takes place when talented students go in for the scientific und professional lines. The residual batch endeavour for the superior civil services. Education services, positions in Commercial and Industrial Organisation etc. Last of all, the remaining unemployable ones apply for Provincial Civil Services as a last resort. So their quality is self-evident. But once employed as "generalists" they under the patronage of their superior "generalists" become fit for running and controlling any organisation dealing with law and order, revenue collection, management of education and scientific, industrial, commercial and agricultural departments, organisations and institutions. [EPESA:1970§8-10]

A doctor entering in service is by-and-large, the best in the academic sense at all levels, matric, intermediate and B.Sc. He takes six years to complete his studies and spends another 6 or 7 years in specialising, competes in a fiercely international examination and then joins up the service at a level and with a sense of progress which can only be termed indiscribably [sic] inferior to a graduate who joins up the Civil Service of Pakistan. Instances are available where two members of the same batch at high school and at college were branched out into medicine and CSP. The member who worked his way through his professional education and found himself on joining the service without even a reasonable quarter to live in whereas the member who was inferior to him in academic works and in education occupying the post of a Deputy Commisioner with all this post means. Examples of highhandedness by far junior people holding executive positions towards far senior doctors are many. [PMA:1970:§3]

A final theme more rarely stated but often implicit in the service association demands is the argument that the CSP as a cadre is responsible for the ills which beset the administrative system of Pakistan. A particularly vituperative, though not unrepresentative statement of this argument is found in the petition of the Pakistan Association of Electrical and Mechanical Engineers:

1. Instead of remaining an impartial administrative machinery, it [the CSP] had taken over the policies of the country against all aspirations of the people.
2. Instead of keeping the judiciary independent, it involved itself into judiciary as well, particularly at the District and Divisional levels.
3. Instead of playing the role of *Civil Servants*, they had become the *masters* of the people by the misuse of the authority of maintaining law and order.
4. Instead of leaving the policy making and execution of the professional services in the hands of respective professionals, the CSPs had monopolised all policy making and execution authority resulting in the problems of teachers, students, doctors, engineers, workers, farmers, industrialists, agriculturalists, commerce, and *under productivity* all over. [PAEME:1970:Annexure A, §1-4]

In sum then, these themes can be said to express one general argument, namely, that generalist cadres, (particularly the CSP), constitute an undeserved elite within the bureaucracy of Pakistan. Conversely, technocrats equally or more deserving than generalists are denied senior positions within the bureaucracy. Not surprisingly, the policy recommendations made by the physicians and engineers were crafted to remedy these perceived injustices.

Policy Recommendations of Technocrats

An analysis of the nineteen service association demands cited above [see page 153] reveals seven "mainstream" policy positions held in common by the majority of such associations.[17]

1) *Reservation of posts should be discontinued.* The practice of the legal reservation of posts within the central secretariat for members of favored generalist cadres, (particularly the CSP), should be discontinued. All posts should be open to all public servants on the basis of merit or suitability of appointment.

2) *Remuneration of officers on the basis of cadre affiliation should be discontinued.* Separate pay scales determined by cadre affiliation and skewed to favor members of particular elite cadres, (particularly the CSP), should be abolished and replaced with a uniform national pay scale. Remuneration should be based on qualifications/skills not on cadre affiliation.

3) *The All-Pakistan Services should be abolished.* The All-Pakistan Services, (CSP and Police Service of Pakistan), services with constitutionally mandated advantages and protections, should be abolished and should be replaced with a single unified civil service. The new organization should be composed of sub-cadres of all Class I officers. Technocrat cadres, (though there is a great deal of disagreement as to particulars), should be favored and made part of the uniform system.

4) *The CSP should be abolished.* The CSP as an institution should be abolished and its members scattered to sub-cadres or retired from service.

5) *The status of technical officers should be enhanced.* Relevant ministries and departments should be headed by specialists or professionals.

6) *The secretariat system of bureaucratic authority should be modified.* The distinction between staff and line officers should either be discontinued or where continued should be reorganized so that heads of departments are afforded roughly comparable status to secretaries.

7) *Technocrats should be encouraged/allowed to hold general administrative/policy making posts.* The movement of line officers to central secretariat postings should be part of normal career mobility.

III. What the Technocrats Got: The Formulation and Implementation of the Administrative Reforms of 1973

Four years later a civilian regime emerged in Pakistan imbued with the motivation to reform the bureaucracy. Though it is naive to suggest that Prime Minister Bhutto's motivation to reform the bureaucracy stemmed solely from an impartial desire to improve the administration of the state, or to improve the career prospects of technocrats, [Burki:1980; Kennedy:1982(3)] it certainly is the case that the reforms incorporated a large portion of the demands voiced by technocrats. Indeed the rationale for introducing administrative reforms in Pakistan reads as if it could have been borrowed directly from numerous physician and/or engineering service association demands. Two themes predominate. First is the argument that the bureaucracy is a legacy of the colonial past, unsuited to the needs of a free, democratic people:

> The bureaucracy we inherited at the time of Partition was designed by the East India Company to serve as the agent of imperialism in the subcontinent. Today the situation is different. The people through their elected representatives are now in power. The people need, indeed demand, a new system of administration. A strong, honest and professionally competent administration that is clean, accountable to the people and wholeheartedly dedicated to the development of the country and the people. [GOP, Ministry of Information and Broadcasting:1975:13-4]

Similarly:

> No institution in the country has so lowered the quality of our national life as what is called 'Naukarshahi'. It has done so by imposing a caste system on our society. It has created a class of Brahmins or Mandarins, unrivalled in its snobbery and arrogance, insulated from the life of the people and incapable of identifying with them. [GOP, Ministry of Information and Broadcasting:1975:13]

The second theme argues that the administrative system simply does not work effectively or efficiently. For example:

> Who can deny that the system breeds widespread corruption and inefficiency? Who can ignore the fact that it causes a hardening of the arteries of Government? A People's Government cannot tolerate the unrestrained individualism, the exclusive concern for self-promotion and the consequent lack of devoted team-work which can be observed throughout the different levels of the administrative structure. It cannot condone a system which elevates the "generalist" above the scientist, the technician, the professional expert, the artist or the teacher. It cannot be indifferent to the fact that the decision-making process has a clerical orientation, that Parkinson's Law operates without impediment, that there is a total absence of a scientific career management and that the resources of local government are not utilised in full measure. If we are to speed the development of our country, if we wish to bring about a closer rapport between officials and the people, if we are to mobilize the nation's talent for the task of government, we have to overhaul the existing structure. [GOP, Ministry of Information and Broadcasting:1975:13-4]

Similarly, the specific recommendations mirror many of the recommendations expressed by the technocrats. The salient provisions of the reform as announced in late 1973 were:[18]

> (1). All service cadres were abolished, and were replaced by a reorganized system of occupational "groups". In addition, service associations were disbanded, and the use of service designations following officer's names was prohibited.
> (2). The existence of different pay scales for different cadres was abolished and was replaced with a uniform National Pay Scale.
> (3). The long-standing practice of reserving certain posts in the central secretariat for officers who were members of elite cadres was discontinued.
> (4). A program of joint pre-service training was established. The Civil Service Academy was disbanded and was replaced by the Academy for Administrative Training.
> (5). Provision was made for the induction of "lateral recruits", into the central secretariat.

As is readily apparent, the Government's mechanisms designed to enhance the career prospects of technocrats envisaged a combination of the abolition of reserved posts for generalist cadres and the provision of "lateral recruitment". Noteworthy is the fact that none of the nineteen physician and engineering service associations had proposed the latter policy. Indeed, "lateral recruitment" may have been the exclusive brainchild of Prime Minister Bhutto. [Kennedy:1980:43] In any event, the implementation of the lateral recruitment program became the cornerstone of administrative reform directly applicable to technocrats. While the program was in fullswing, (1973-1975), 60 technical officers[19] were selected to join the federal bureaucracy—11.5% of the total number of lateral recruits selected. (See Table Two). With regard to the Secretariat Group, the majority of technical officers selected through lateral recruitment were engineers who had previously held non-cadre government appointments. Of the 50 technical officers selected for the Secretariat Group, 33 were trained engineers[20] and 48 were public servants.[21] Only one lateral recruit was trained in medicine.

Table 2

*Occupational Specialty of Lateral Recruits to the
Federal Bureaucracy of Pakistan**

Occupation	Group of Assignment				
	Sec. G.	FAG	TAG	DMG	Totals
Public Administration	69(22.8)	18(12.9)	--	2(33.3)	89(18.3)
District Administration	17(5.6)	10(7.1)	--	1(16.7)	28(5.7)
Finance	90(29.7)	8(5.7)	--	--	98(20.1)
Law	21(6.9)	24(17.1)	--	--	45(9.2)
Business Administration	7(2.3)	10(7.1)	--	--	17(3.5)
Military	17(5.6)	25(17.9)	38(100)	3(50)	83(17.0)
Education	33(10.9)	28(20.0)	--	--	61(12.5)
Arts	19	17	--	--	36
Social Sciences	8	7	--	--	15
Natural Sciences	6	4	--	--	10
Journalism	2(.7)	9(6.4)	--	--	11(2.3)
Agriculture	3(1)	2(1.4)	--	--	5(1.0)
Medicine	1(.3)	--	--	--	1(.2)
Technical/Scientific	43(14.2)	6(4.3)	--	--	49(10.1)
Missing	21	6	--	--	27
Total	324	146	38	6	514

(Figures in parentheses are adjusted frequencies of total, deleting missing data)

ᴬThe categories of occupation were defined by the author after exploring available information for each recruit. Since recruits often had diverse backgrounds, we chose to present the "dominant background", of the candidates.

Source: [Kennedy:1980:47-50]

Table 3

Technical Lateral Recruits to Secretariat Group
by Occupational Specialty 1973-82

Occupation	Selected 1973-5	In Service 1976	In Service 1982
Engineers	33	32	18
Natural Science	16	4	1
Medicine	1	1	1
Totals	50	36	20

Source: Compiled by the author from GOP, Establishment Division:1976; GOP, Establishment Division:1978; GOP, Establishment Division:1982; numerous administrative memoranda; and interviews.

Subsequent to 1975 the avenue of lateral recruitment was blocked. Two rationales explain its discontinuance. First, the Government found it increasingly difficult to absorb the large number of officers being inducted under the terms of the lateral recruitment program. Simply put, the Government did not need more personnel. Second, the Program was not popular among orthodox direct-entry bureaucrats. Almost universally such officers complained that lateral recruits had either blocked their prospects for promotion and/or were not competent to handle posts to which they had been assigned. Also, lateral recruits were perceived as political appointees, at best undeserving of their bureaucratic assignment, at worst "spies" of the Government. [Kennedy:1980:59-60] After the military coup of 1977 which toppled Mr. Bhutto, the military regime was quick to further discredit the Program [e.g. GOP:1979] and officers who had been selected by the Program had to pass the scrutiny of a Review Board designed to ferret out political irregularities. Though most technical officers passed this Board, it is worth noting that of the 50 technically-trained lateral recruits selected for the Program only 20 remained in service by 1982. (See Table Three).

The effect of other provisions of the administrative reform [see above] also had important consequences for the status of technocrats. On the positive side, the abolition of cadre-based pay schedules and the establishment of a uniform pay scale served to increase the pay of technocrats as well as meeting the long-standing demands for the induction of MBBS and BS(Eng) as Class I (NPS 17) officers. Less positive in the long term has been the abolition of service cadres. The net effect of this provision was to replace generalist cadres "services" with functionally-analogous "groups". But, for technical services no "groups" have been allowed to replace the now-defunct Central Engineering Service, the T + T Service, nor the several provincial physician and engineering services. This latter outcome has hampered the organizational capabilities of technocrats and has lessened their inter-institutional clout.

IV. What the Technocrats Still Want: 1982 and Beyond

Despite the not insignificant gains of 1973-5, technocrats have remained dissatisfied with their place in the bureaucratic system of Pakistan. And during the last eighteen months technocrats have once again taken to the streets to demonstrate their displeasure. Seemingly the most disaffected group has been the so-called "junior doctors", (hospital staff physicians holding only an MBBS degree). This group, spearheaded by the Pakistan Doctor's Organisation (PDO), participated in a brief nationwide strike in March, 1981. The strike was contained when the Government appointed the Jogezai Committee to look into the doctor's grievances. But due to the lack of concrete Government action to meet their demands and the failure to release the findings of the Committee, the grievances redoubled in intensity and found expression in the episodic physician strikes of March-June, 1982.[22] It is claimed that nearly 4000 doctors participated in the strikes which were observed in the Punjab, Sind and the NWFP. The dominant technique employed was a work slowdown in which striking staff physicians failed to show up for work three days a week-Sunday, Monday, and Tuesday. There were also reported instances in which physicians refused to perform routine surgery or to make regular rounds of the wards. [*Muslim*:June 8, 1982] The response of the Government was a combination of the carrot and the stick. The "stick" included the detention of 70 striking physicians in the NWFP, [*Mulim*:June 22, 1982] the termination of the services of 30 junior doctors in the Punjab, [*Muslim*:June 23, 1982] and the compulsory transfer of several hundred recalcitrant doctors during the summer. The "carrot" was the promise held out by the Government of assured employment, increased promotional prospects, and increased pay. [*Muslim*:June 23, 1982]

The junior doctor's demands were primarily centered on the issue of promotional prospects for staff physicians. Junior duty medical officers possess a terminal MBBS degree and typically hold posts at NPS Grades 17 and 18. Except for the relatively few posts open to such officers in hospital administration, posts of NPS Grades 19 and above are reserved for physicians with advanced degrees. Therefore, the bulk of junior doctors face relatively limited career prospects. Such limitations are particularly galling to junior physicians who often perform the same hospital duties as senior physicians and who are also predominantly excluded from the often lucrative private medical practices of senior colleagues. It is also galling to junior physicians to be effectively excluded from the more sanguine career prospects of generalist officers. The remedy for these ills, many junior doctors argue, is the establishment of a "Central Medical Cadre"—in the words of one prominent striking physician crafted to be "analogous to the CSP". Another remedy supported by many physicians is to limit the number of students admitted to medical colleges. Also mentioned occasionally as a remedy is the reintroduction of lateral recruitment.

Less dramatic, though nonetheless strident, have been the demands of the engineers. Indeed, engineering groups have the well-deserved reputation of being the most feisty intra-bureaucratic actors in Pakistan. Two major demands have been voiced by engineering associations during the last year: (1) The establishment of a cadre of engineers, "The Ministry of Engineering Affairs", and (2) the reintroduction of lateral recruitment. The first demand foresees the establishment of a giant cadre which incorporates the 7000-odd officer-level engineers working in various governmental and semi-governmental capacities. This cadre, which would be comprised of approximately one-half of all officers in the federal bureaucracy of Pakistan, would be sub-divided into ten subcadres: Water and power, communications, production, railways, housing and works, petroleum and natural resources, industries, science and technology, defense production, and aviation. The movement of officers between subcadres would be encouraged but career planning and personnel policy would be handled by the central ministry, ostensibly staffed exclusively by engineers. The second demand, somewhat less grandiose, is that engineers holding comparable posts should be inducted into the Secretariat Group. In 1982 only 8 of the 130 NPS Grades 21 and 22, (additional secretaries and secretaries), in the Secretariat Group were trained engineers. [GOP: Establishment Division:1982] This under representation could be remedied by a massive influx of lateral recruits. Accordingly, the names of 188 engineers were recently recommended by the Pakistan Engineering Council for entry into the Secretariat Group, (Grades 19-22). Similarly, the Pakistan Engineering Council has also recommended that most, (17 of 19), federal secretary posts and 45 secretary-level posts in autonomous corporations be reserved for engineers. [Pakistan Engineering Council:1982]

The Government of Pakistan has found it difficult, if not impossible, to fully meet the demands of the disaffected physicians and engineers. First, in regard to physician demands, the response has been to create new posts, to upgrade existing posts, [*Muslim*: June 22, 1982] and to undertake preliminary studies on how to tighten admission standards to medical colleges. [*Muslim*: June 28, 1982] However, the major demand, namely the creation of a separate cadre with favored terms and conditions of service is not likely to be met because in the words of one government official, "the Government cannot upset the entire economic structure merely to favor one professional group". Unfortunately, given the rapid proliferation of demands for increased medical admissions, coupled with the attendant underemployment of new graduates, and the dislocations caused by a more bullish market for medical talent abroad, one can safely assume that the demands of junior doctors are likely to become increasingly insistent and perforce even more difficult for the Government to dodge.

Of course, the Government has had even greater difficulty meeting the "radical" demands of disaffected engineers. The proposal to establish the Ministry of Engineering Affairs was summarily rejected with a rationale reminiscent of technocratic critiques of generalist administration. Perhaps, ironically, the Government rejected the establishment of the Ministry on the grounds that "engineering" encompasses very disparate occupations and therefore cannot logically or efficiently be subsumed under one authority. The response to the demand for the induction of 188 engineers into the Secretariat Group has been met with a subcontinental Catch-22. Engineers who work in autonomous corporations are not by definition members of the "civil services", therefore they cannot be considered for appointment to a group for which civil servant status is requisite. And since the abrogation of the lateral recruitment program there is no mechanism for converting non-civil servants into civil servants. However, the relevant issue is not whether engineers become members of the Secretariat Group, but rather whether engineers can gain access to secretariat appointments, by definition the preserve of members of the Secretariat Group.

In conclusion this paper has demonstrated three lessons concerning the relationship between technocrats and generalists in the Pakistani administration. Undoubtedly, all three lessons are applicable in various contexts to other bureaucratic systems.

(1) *Institutional history is important.* Given the historical legacy and current structure of the bureaucratic system of Pakistan one inescapable conclusion is that the rules of the game are stacked to favor generalist administrators over technocrats. More importantly, once the rules have been set, as they were for Pakistan arguably as early as the mid-nineteenth century, they are hard to change. Consequently, technocrats attempting to break into the system face two formidable hurdles: (a) They must demonstrate extraordinary personal competence—after all "technocrats are not good administrators", and (b), they must overcome bureaucratic norms and practices designed to favor generalists.

(2) *The relationship between generalist and technocrat is zero-sum.* Technocrats and generalists are competing for the same set of jobs. As a consequence a gain by a technocrat is offset by a loss to a generalist. Though this may be an over-simplified view of the process, such perceptions provide potent imagery for both sets of actors.

(3) *There is no easy solution.* In Pakistan the battle between technocrat and generalist has raged since Partition and there is no indication that it will end soon. Perhaps the interests of the groups are inherently irreconcilable. Certain, however, is the fact that external pressures will exacerbate such differences within Pakistan in the future. Both physicians and engineers face underemployment at home and a burgeoning, if episodic, demand for their services abroad. The uncertainties caused by such a confluence of factors are likely to make both sides intensify or radicalize their struggle. The evidence provided by the Disturbances of 1968-9 and by the recent junior physician strike lend credence to this hypothesis. Also important to note is that the demands of disaffected groups in 1982 are more maximalist than analogous demands in 1969. The sides are further apart. Our reluctant forecast therefore is for more of the same—increasing politicization of both sides, episodic strikes and likely violence.

NOTES

The author wishes to gratefully acknowledge the support received from the American Institute of Pakistan Studies, (1975-6), and, (1982), which made field research in Pakistan and this paper possible. I also wish to thank Bowdoin College - particularly the Faculty Development Fund and the Department of Government. Finally, I wish to thank Ms. Ann M. Sargent for her help in data collation.

1   For the purposes of this paper the term "technocrat" refers to physicians and engineers employed in the public service of Pakistan. This accords with the usage of the term in Pakistan. Physicians and engineers constitute the only sizable groupings of technically-trained personnel in the bureaucracy of Pakistan.

2   Technically, subsequent to the reforms of 1973, the term "Central Superior Service" is a misnomer. First, the reforms abolished all services. Second, the former "Central Superior Services" were divided into the All-Pakistan Unified Grades and the Federal Unified Grades. However, the term "CSS Examination" is still universally employed.

3   There are myriad exceptions to this rule which relax the age limits upward for certain categories of recruits. Groups subject to these extended limits include: scheduled castes, Buddhists, individuals domiciled in designated "tribal areas", military personnel, and most recently, individuals from certain under represented provinces.

4   The CSS Examination was "combined" for recruitment to all services from 1949 to 1956. In 1957, a short-lived experiment, ostensibly designed to afford candidates an opportunity to express an early choice of group preference, was attempted in which three separate examinations were held—one for the CSP, one of the PSP, and one for the other Central Services. [Government of Pakistan, Federal Public Service Commission:1959] In 1961, this experiment was dropped and the CSS Examination again was combined to recruit all members of the Central Superior Services. [GOP, Central Public Service Commission: 1963] The CSS Examination has remained a vehicle of combined recruitment to the present day.

5   The five-fold division of the compulsory subjects has been constant since the 1967 CSS Examination. Prior to this, three of the five papers were concerned with English and only two with general knowledge. [Bhatti: 1974]

6   Perhaps the best way to experience the flavor of the CSS Examination is to look at the actual questions that have been asked in recent years. The English Essay typically gives the candidate a choice between several themes. Sample themes (1972) include such topics as: "Relevance of Islam to Science", "Sanctity of Law", "Competition or Planned Economy?", "The Sick Soul" etc. English precis and composition inevitably asks the candidate to rephrase a technical paragraph and/or an English poem into everyday English. This part of the exam also often asks candidates to explain the meaning of certain English colloquialisms such as (1970) "to smell a rat", "sour grapes", "wooly-headed", "feather in his cap" etc. The everyday science exam asks questions which cover the entire range of commonsense interpretations of natural and biological phenomena. Typical examples of such questions include (1974): "How does the sun make a rainbow?"; "In what part of the world are the following found—(i) chamois, (ii) elk, (iii) llama, (iv) moose, and (v) reindeer?"; "How can bats fly in the dark?" etc. The current affairs section usually asks questions concerned with international politics. Questions asked cover the sort of information commonly found in publications such as *Time* and *Newsweek*. As a consequence, candidates often spend a considerable portion of their study hours reading such periodicals. [Bhatti:1974; Bhatti:1982]

7   In the 1978 CSS Examination forty-nine optional subjects were available for candidate selection though only thirty-three were actually offered by candidates. The most popular offerings (100 or more candidates selected them) were in order of preference: Islamic History and Culture (552), History of Pakistan and India (401), Political Science (296), Constitutional Law (204), Urdu (189), Muslim Civil Law and Jurisprudence (186), Economics (166), International Relations (147), and Law (105). [GOP, Federal Public Service Commission: 1982:99-101]

8   Before 1973 successful candidates for the CSS Examination were assigned on the basis of that examination and by individual preference directly to services. Depending on which group the probationer was assigned to, probationers often underwent additional training. The more notable training institutions of this latter type were the Civil Service Academy (for the CSP and FSP), the Police Training Institute (PSP), and the Finance Services Academy (PAAS, PMAS, PRAS, PCES). In 1973 the Civil Service Academy and the Finance Services Academy were merged to form the Academy for Administrative Training. Doors to the new Academy were opened on December 1, 1973. In 1980, the process reverted to the pre-1973 pattern with assignment to a group made immediately subsequent to the results of the CSS Examination, though combined joint training of all successful CSS probationers was continued. Also, the Academy for Administrative Training was renamed the Civil Services Academy.

9   Comprehensive information is not available for batches subsequent to 1976. However, the assertions made below regarding 1970-1976 remain valid for 1977-1980. [GOP, Federal Public Service Commission:1982, 1980, 1979]

10   Before 1973 such occupational groups were referred to as "services". [Kennedy:1981]

11   Recruitment to two groups has recently, (1982), been discontinued. The Tribal Areas Group has been merged with the District Management Group and the Office Management Group has simply ceased to exist.

12   The Secretariat Group is a composite group consisting of all Deputy Secretaries NPS Grade 19 and above and former CSP officers in Grade 18 working in the federal secretariat. [Kennedy:1981]

13   The CSP, as were all other services, was abolished as a consequence of the administrative reforms of 1973. Most such services were replaced with functionally-analogous groups. The CSP was replaced by the District Management Group and the Tribal Areas Group. [Kennedy:1981]

14   In all, disregarding cases of personal grievance, there were 1051 petitions addressed to the Committee; in excess of 200 of these documents were official representations of service associations.

15   Central Engineering Service Association (CES), East Pakistan Engineer's Service Association (EPESA), TIP Junior and Senior Engineer's Association-East Pakistan, Civil Aviation Engineer's Association, Telegraph and Telephone Engineering Service, East Pakistan (T + T), East Pakistan Water and Power Development Authority Engineer's Association (EPWAPDA), West Pakistan Water and Power Development Authority Engineer's Association (WPWAPDA), The Institute of Engineers-Dacca, East Pakistan University of Engineering and Technology Teachers Association, West Pakistan Service of Engineers (Electricity Department), Pakistan Association of Electrical and Mechanical Engineers (PAEME), Electrical Engineer's Association-Lahore, Punjab Gazetted Engineer's Association, Pakistan Society of Public Health Engineers, and Material Technologists and Engineer's Association P.C.S.I.R.-Lahore.

16   Pakistan Medical Association (PMA), West Pakistan Health Service Association (WPHSA), Medical Doctors in Central Government Employment Association (Central Doctors), and East Pakistan Medical Services Association (EPMSA).

17   Obviously the style and comprehensiveness of service association demands vary. The policy recommendations which follow are typical of the service association demands as a whole, and though their substance is consistent with the several sets of policy recommendations they are not directly representative of any one service association.

18   The policies contemplated by the reform movement were announced in several places including: [GOP, Ministry of Information and Broadcasting: 12-16; Ghulam Mustafa Jatoi's press statement of August 21, 1973 found in *Pakistan Times* August 22, 1973 and in numerous administrative directives.]

19   "Technical officers" is used broadly here, to refer to physicians, engineers, those trained at the BS level or higher in the natural sciences, and all individuals who had served in a technical capacity for ten years or more prior to selection regardless of college training. Not all of the recruits "selected" were actually inducted into the service. See Table Three.

20   "Trained" means holding at least the BS(Eng) degree. Four of these officers also held advanced degrees in engineering, two had Ph.D.s.
21   42 worked for federal or provincial governments, and 6 were faculty or administrators at government colleges. The remaining two were in private business.
22   The description presented here has validity only through July, 1982.

REFERENCES

BHATTI, Mohammed Ibrahim
    1982   *CSS Compulsory Question Papers.* , Jhelum, Bhatti Publishers.
    1974   *CSS Compulsory Question Papers.* Jhelum, Bhatti Publishers.
BURKI, Shahid Javed
    1980   *Pakistan Under Bhutto, 1971-1977.* New York, St. Martin's.
    1972   "Ayub's Fall: A Socio-Economic Explanation" *Asian Survey* Vol. XXII.
Government of Pakistan
    1979   *White Paper on the Performance of the Bhutto Regime.* Islamabad, PCPP.
    1971   *Services Reorganisation Committee Report, 1969-70.* A. R. Cornelius chairman. Islamabad, MPCPP.
Government of Pakistan, Cabinet Secretariat
    1969   *Report of the Pay and Services Commission, 1959-1962.* A. R. Cornelius chairman. Karachi, MPCPP.
Government of Pakistan, Central Public Service Commission
    1963   *Annual Report for the Year 1962.* Karachi, MGP.
Government of Pakistan, Civil Services Academy
    1980   "Course of Study" (photostat).
Government of Pakistan, Establishment Division
    1982   *Provisional Gradation List of Officers of the All-Pakistan Unified Grades, 1982* (photostat).
    1978   *Provisional Gradation List of Officers of the All-Pakistan Unified Grades, 1978* (photostat).
    1976   *Provisional Gradation List of Officers of the All-Pakistan Unified Grades, 1975* (photostat).
Government of Pakistan, Federal Public Service Commission
    1982   *Annual Report 1980.* Islamabad, MPCPP.
    1980   *Annual Report for the Year 1979.* Islamabad, MPCPP.
    1979   *Annual Report for the Year 1978.* Islamabad, MPCPP.
    1978   *Annual Report for the Year 1977.* Islamabad, MPCPP.
    1976   *Combined Competitive Engineering Examination.* Karachi, MGP.
    1959   *Annual Report for the Year 1958.* Karachi, MGP.
Government of Pakistan, Ministry of Information and Broadcasting
    1975   *Speeches and Statements of Zulfikar Ali Bhutto Prime Minister of Pakistan, August 14-December 31, 1973.* Karachi, MPCPP.
Government of Pakistan, O + M Division
    1981   *Report of the Sixth Triennial Census of Federal Government Civil Servants as on 1st January 1980.* Islamabad, O + M Division.
Government of Pakistan, O + M Wing
    1975   *Provisional Data on Distribution of Employees of Autonomous/Semi-Autonomous Organizations and Taken Over Establishments, ...,* 1-11-74. Rawalpindi, O + M Wing.
Great Britain, Parliament
    1876   "Report on the Indian Civil Service 1854" in *Parliamentary Papers* Vol. LV.
    1853   *Hansard's Parliamentary Debates* Vol. CXXVII (June 24).
HEEGER, Gerald
    1977   "Politics in the Post-Military State: Some Reflections on the Pakistani Experience" *World Politics* XXIX.
HUSAIN, Agha Iftikhar
    1979   *Studies in Public Administration of Pakistan* (Islamabad, Pakistan Administrative Research Centre).

KENNEDY, Charles H.
  1982(3) "Policy Formulation in Pakistan: Antecedents to Bhutto's Administrative Reforms" *Journal of Commonwealth and Comparative Politics* Vol. XX no. 1.
  1982(2) "Affirmative Action in Pakistan" (19th Northeastern Political Science Meeting, New Haven).
  1982(1) "The Quota System of Regional Representation in Pakistan" (11th Conference on South Asia, Madison).
  1981 "Policy Implementation: The Case of Structural Reforms in the Administrative System of Pakistan" *Journal of South Asian and Middle Eastern Studies* Vol. IV no. 3.
  1980 "Analysis of the Lateral Recruitment Program to the Federal Bureaucracy of Pakistan 1973-79" *Journal of South Asian and Middle Eastern Studies* Vol. III no. 4.
  1979 *The Context, Content, and Implementation of Bhutto's Administrative Reforms in Pakistan.* Durham, Duke University Ph.D.
MUNEER, Ahmed
  1978 *Political Sociology: Perspectives on Pakistan.* Lahore, Punjab Abdi Markaz.
Muslim
  1982 May-August.
Pakistan Engineering Council.
  1982 *Job Analysis of Senior Management Posts Under Federal Government and Corporations.* Islamabad, Pakistan Engineering Council.
Pakistan Times
  1969 January-March.
  1968 November-December.
SAYEED, Khalid bin
  1979 "Mass Urban Protests as Indicators of Political Change in Pakistan" *Journal of Commonwealth and Comparative Politics* Vol. XVII.
SRINIVAS, S. N.
  1967 *Social Change in Modern India.* Berkeley, University of California.

The Techno-Managerial and Politico-Managerial Classes in a Milk Cooperative of India

A. H. SOMJEE

Simon Fraser University, Burnaby, Canada

THE BURGEONING MILK cooperatives of India—which are now regarded by experts on rural development as one of the major success stories, and whose assistance is being sought by other developing countries through the World Bank—indicate the presence of a complex but complementary relationship, with limited frictions, between their techno-managerial class and the politico-managerial class. Both these classes, apart from the technocratic and political nature of their work, are also involved in *managerial* activity where problems of jurisdiction and ultimate preponderance in crucial decisions can make or mar the succes of any organization. Both these classes in their actual operational involvement, despite occasional and sometimes persistent lapses in certain fields, have shown a remarkable sense of accommodation, need for concession, and foresight in terms of what will ultimately benefit the average milk producer in the district. While there is much greater evidence of such an operational relationship within the milk cooperatives of Gujarat, where cooperative dairying, based on grass roots involvement, began, there is also a growing body of evidence that a cooperative approach is slowly gaining ground elsewhere despite great odds.

Within such cooperative organizations these two classes, whom we shall refer to as "technocrats" and "politicians" for the sake of convenience, jointly become involved in a wide range of activities. Together they build, operate, expand, and replicate complex organizations involving a large number of people and resources.

In this paper we shall concentrate on the problem of interdependence, jurisdiction, concession, preponderance, and friction within the relationships between the technocrats and politicians. For this purpose we shall examine the relationship between the two classes within India's premier milk cooperative, namely AMUL.[1]

The paper is divided into the following parts: (i) the background of the dairy cooperative movement; (ii) the interdependency of technologists and politicians; and, (iii) political stresses and strains. We shall now examine each of these parts in some detail.

(i) *Background of Dairy Cooperative Movement*

AMUL milk cooperative, in a real sense of the term, is an offshoot of the Indian national movement. In its establishment, and later on in its organization and development, major national political figures such as Sardar Patel and Morarji Desai, and, at the district level, Tribhuvandas Patel (TK) were deeply involved. The groundwork for a cooperative organization, which was meant to protect the average milk producer at the village level from the ruthless milk traders, was laid by nationalist leaders, and even when the technologists subsequently joined them, the philosophy, and direction of the organization continued to be that which was given by the original leaders. Its technologists, while building, operating, and replicating similar organizations elsewhere in India, never lost sight of the social concerns of the nationalists for protecting the rural poor. They worked with the politicians of the post-independence era, who were several cuts below the nationalist leaders in their integrity and social concerns, and they brought to bear the fruits of their ability to build and run complex organizations, to introduce the modern technology of dairying and the science of cattle improvement, and above all to launch effective marketing approaches—all these, in order to be able to secure the maximum return for the average milk producer. Without them and their organizational effort the average milk producer at the village level was defenceless. In addition, for both the technologists and politicians the building and operating of large scale milk cooperatives was a great learning experience.

Initially, the major advantage of these developers was that they chose to build a milk cooperative in a district such as Kaira which had one of the largest milk resource potentials in the country. But to bring the milk producers of the district within one cooperative organization, of which neither they nor the organizers had any prior experience, was indeed a remarkable achievement. Towards this the presence of an agriculturist caste in the district, namely, the Patidars—which was known to be innovative by nature and receptive to new ideas—proved to be of inestimable value. While the technocrats and politicians were struggling with the refinement of the form which the new organization should take, the Patidar milk producers of the village, with their willingness to try out anything new and different,[2] went ahead with minimum direction and reported back their priceless operating experience in running the new organization. After that the founders of AMUL had much less difficulty in extending the network of their organization to other parts of the district.

Historically speaking, the milk producers of the district had for a long time made use of the surplus milk to make *ghee* (purified butter). It was then sold to the *ghee* traders in the town of Mahemdabad,[3] who in turn sold it to traders in cities such as Bombay and Ahmedabad. The major share of money went to the traders in Mahemdabad and the town thus became the *ghee* marketing centre of the region.

Technology hit the milk trade of the distinct in the later half of the nineteenth century when a businessman from the village Nar brought in an imported cream separator from Bombay. Later on a similar machine, despite all the crudities, was indigenously made. The cream separator changed the nature of the milk trade in the district. It also adversely affected the flourishing *ghee* trade in the region. Later on, it gave rise to big milk dairies in the cities of Bombay and Ahmedabad.

The British army needed a steady supply of milk and milk products, which in turn created the need for the rationalization of the milk business. Such an effort gave rise to a new breed of middlemen in the milk business who sought official protection and exclusive rights to receive milk from the producers.

In order to ensure a steady supply of milk and milk products, a government-run central creamery was established in the city of Bombay. After that more creameries were created in the milk surplus district of Kaira to make sure that the Bombay government creamery and its dependent British army did not go without milk or milk products.

The intervention on the part of government in the milk business created a flourishing class of milk traders and milk product manufacturers. Such a class was known in the district as the *sanchawallas* (those who operated machines). They dictated the price of the milk, and the farmer, who had no other recourse, had to accept it. After separating the cream from the milk, the *sachawallas* used to throw away the residue in the village streets leaving behind a dried trail of white liquid in one rural community after another. The mode of production based on cream separators thus wasted all other properties in the milk except fat. And to that extent, in what was a monopoly situation, the producers got very little in return on what they offered. An Englishman from Warrickshire, called Reeves, who ran his own milk diary in the town of Nadiad, appropriately called this period in the dairy industry an "era of waste".

Soon another wave of technological development hit the milk industry this time directed at the other ingredient left out in the fatless milk, namely, casein. In 1911, a German technologist called Kohler came out with a method of extracting casein from the residual milk. Kohler was invited to a village in the district called Samarkha by an enterprising silk merchant to set up an industrial unit to extract casein. A Parsi gentleman called Banker also joined them. Initially Kohler got the fatless milk free of charge, but when he started extracting casein from it, the price went up. Consequently, Kohler made an arrangement to receive whole milk so that he could get both cream and casein out of it. Such an arrangement from his point of view was much more economical. The prominent milk traders who supplied him with milk were known as Doshi Brothers.

Kohler kept strictly to himself the simple technology of casein-making. He regularly mixed some kind of an unknown chemical with milk but would not tell anyone what it was. Moreover, he made all his employees sign an undertaking that they would not start a rival casein-making factory of their own. While his employees knew the mechanical, and to some extent the chemical, process involved, they did not know what kind of secret chemical Kohler used in the final mix in order to get casein. For the purposes of mixing the mysterious chemical, he had trained a special assistant called Mansukhlal Kapasi. But Kapasi was not as trustworthy as Kohler believed. In Kohler's absence, he once deliberately refrained from mixing the mysterious chemical and still casein came out at the other end of the manufacturing process. Kapasi was now convinced that Kohler, the great technologist, had fooled everyone. What Kohler had in fact used was water given the slightly misleading smell of a chemical.

After that, Kapasi, approached various firms to which Kohler supplied casein and quoted a much lower price for it. When Kohler came to know about it, he brought his gun, shot at Kapasi, and missed. Later on Kohler filed a suit and Kapasi was sentenced to two months' imprisonment for the breach of his undertaking. The higher court, however, reversed the decision, and thus ended the cloak-and-dagger phase of technology in the Indian milk industry.

Subsequently Kapasi started his own creamery and casein manufacturing company at Anand. With the declaration of the First World War, Kohler was locked up as an enemy alien. His partners, however, continued his business until 1921. Since there were too many casein makers in the district, Kohler's firm could not stand the competition and finally folded up.

During the First World War there came on the scene yet another industrial entrepreneur in the milk industry, namely, Pestonji Polson, the maker of the famous Polson Butter, who established the first modern dairy for milk products. He too owed his rise to the shortage of dairy products in the dining halls of the British army. An army officer in charge of food supplies, named Col. Dickson, persuaded Pestonji Polson to set up a mechanized unit at Anand so that the army might get an uninterrupted supply of butter after the war.

Before entering into the butter-making business, Pestonji Edulji Dalal, later known as Pestonji Polson, used to sell, in Bombay's Crawford Market, what he called "French Coffee" which was a blend of coffee and chicory. The armed forces needed coffee in large quantity and Pestonji was therefore able to do a roaring business for himself. His coffee business brought him in close contact with Col. Dickson and other officers who gave him the nickname of "Polly". When he "hit the big time" as a supplier of coffee, and later on of butter, these army officials persuaded him to change his name to Pestonji Polson, with Polson as the brand name of his product. Thus was born a respectable-sounding trade name, because of the sheer need of the alien armed forces for the mechanically produced butter. During this time no one paid any attention to the condition of the average milk producer nor to the portion of money from the sale of milk and milk products that actually reached him.

The highly mechanized dairy at Anand started functioning in 1929. Between 1929 and 1939, Polson vastly increased the production of cream, butter, and casein, and some of his products were even exported to the countries of Southeast Asia and Africa.

In 1934, Polson established a pasteurization plant at Anand, the only one of its kind in the east. As a result Polson's organization was known as Polson Model Dairy. The outbreak of the Second Great War once again boosted

Polson's fortune, and during that period its production of butter reached the record high of three million pounds a year.

Despite the fact that Polson Dairy provided the farmers with a muchneeded and assured market for their milk, the cash return did not register any significant increase. What is more, the farmers were even deprived of the freedom to sell milk to any other organization.

In 1945, in order to remove the perennial shortage of milk, the then Government of Bombay came out with a milk scheme of its own. By means of such a scheme, it put a ban on the sale of milk and milk products outside the Kaira district. Moreover, it gave a virtual monopoly of milk collection to Polson Dairy in Anand and neighbouring areas. This was the last straw for farmers and political leaders in the area.

Sardar Vallabhbhai Patel, the towering Indian nationalist leader, who came from a village called Karamsad, three miles from Anand, had been toying with the idea of starting a milk cooperative since 1942 but had been far too busy with more important matters such as the organization of the Indian National Congress and the conduct of the freedom movement itself. Moreover, since the declaration of the Quit India Movement, during the same year, he was frequently in prison.

For its part, Polson Dairy was too closely identified with the alien rule and its war efforts. And what was worse, it was trying to meet the requirements of the *raj* with the help of the resources of the Kaira district, the heartland of nationalist political agitation in the region.

In 1946, when Indian independence appeared to be a highly improbable outcome, Sardar Patel, then recently released from prison, and his associates such as Morarji Desai and TK, together with several other political workers, organized what was known as "the 14 villages' Satyagraha", and launched their highly effective non-cooperation movement by not selling milk to Polson Dairy. During the course of the movement, some of the leaders of the district were arrested by the Government of Bombay. However, the same government later on conceded the demand of the political agitators for a milk cooperative organization. The result was that on December 14, 1946, a milk cooperative known as Anand Milk Union Ltd. came into existence. Popularly known as AMUL, this cooperative was destined to become one of the greatest and most prestigious cooperatives in the world.

The fact that AMUL was so closely associated with the topmost nationalist leaders of India, at the very height of the freedom movement, gave assurance that the farmers in the district would mobilize seriously and effectively in support of such a cooperative enterprise. Beyond this success was achieved by means of highly effective organization, technology, animal health care, marketing, high returns, and a rare example of understanding and teamwork between the techno-managerial and the politico-managerial personnel. All other and later successful milk cooperatives of India, studiously followed the organization, technological and political pattern established by AMUL. We now turn to an examination of some aspects of this pattern.

(ii) *Interdependence of Technocrats and Politicians*

In organizing, operating, and extending milk cooperatives the technocrats and politicians had to depend on each other. In the evolution of their interdependence the top men on both sides, i.e., technocrats (managing director and his senior associates), and politicians (chairman and board of directors) played a vital role. They set the pattern of mutual cooperation, implicitly understood the unstated boundaries of jurisdiction, and tacitly agreed to subordinate and superordinate positions and decisions in specific areas where both groups were equally involved.

Since the actual operation of a dairy organization was a matter of management and engineering upkeep, the technologists assumed an important role in it. Moreover, unlike the politicians, whose electoral and party fortunes changed all the time, the technologists were immune from such uncertainties. Consequently, the latter, if they chose, always had the scope and opportunity to consolidate their position and strength, vis-a-vis the impermanent group of politicians. Being relatively more secure in their positions than the politicians, the technocrats often cultivated effective links of communication with the bureaucracy and with politicians at the state level and with New Delhi. Such links also helped them to bypass the district level politicians in certain matters. At the same time, however, in matters of general policy they had to live within the framework of certain politically-motivated decisions imposed by the politicians despite their assured ascendancy in a wide range of matters pursuant to their relationship.

The initial years of AMUL were fraught with squabbles among the politicians themselves. Apart from their personal rivalry, the result of competition for political power in various public organizations within the district, there were the genuine differences among them on the question of the general direction of the new organization. TK wanted AMUL to become a cooperative organization of the milk producers. In his view, since the organization was for the milk producers, they should have the maximum say at all levels of its organization. Natvarlal Dave (ND), a highly respected district level political worker who even went to prison during "the 14 villages' satyagraha", thought otherwise. ND felt that AMUL should become a cooperative of milk collectors. The dispute went to Morarji Desai for arbitration. Desai favoured TK's position. But the clash did not end there. The hostility between TK and ND started affecting several other organizational decisions. Finally, ND was eased out of the organization and later on from the Congress party itself. After a few years of political wilderness and after experiments in political opposition to the Congress, ND, a freedom fighter, social worker, and a Gujarati literary figure of considerable significance, died a bitterly disappointed man.

The emergence of TK as a major figure in district politics, with all the useful vertical links with politicians in the state and New Delhi, and with the firm belief that the milk producer should be the sole basis of a cooperative organization, was of inestimable value to AMUL. Had the ND style philosophy won out, the nature of the cooperative movement in India would have been very different. It is unlikely that it would have been as effective as it was under the philosophy of a democratically operated milk producers' cooperative which AMUL came to be.

TK's hands were further strengthened by the recruitment of Kurien a brilliant engineer with a gift for building vast organizations on highly pragmatic and workable lines. Kurien brought in his own like-minded associates, and, in particular, H. M. Dalaya. Together, and with their technocratic genius, they translated the hazy, populistic cooperative philosophy of Sardar Patel, Morarji Desai, and TK into an organizational reality of great effectiveness and acclaim.

The infant organization of AMUL received a great boost when the new Government of Bombay, after independence, repealed its contract with the privately run Polson Dairy and asked it, a farmers' cooperative, to supply milk to te city of Bombay.

One of the greatest contributions of TK, the politician, was to play down the role of politicians, including himself, in the day-to-day running of the AMUL dairy. Right from the start he either involved the technocrats in major decisions or left decision-making in important as well as unimportant matters solely to them. In their nearly thirty years of work together, TK rarely interferred with what the technocrats wanted. He even defended them and shielded them from wiley politicians and their politically-motivated schemes. The technocrats, in return, expressed their deep gratitude and proved worthy of his trust by building one of the best-known milk cooperatives in the world.

Under TK, the technocrats came to have a free hand. In 1953 UNICEF, together with New Zealand, offered aid to AMUL in providing free milk to children. In 1955 AMUL earned visibility in the Indian market by bringing out the famous AMUL butter. Later, in 1961, it produced baby food, and in 1962 made cheese out of buffalo milk which the experts thought was not possible. Subsequently, it added other products such as *ghee*, milk powder, high protein food, chocolate, etc., and became a household word throughout the entire country.

In company with its own expansion, AMUL continued to provide various benefits for the farmers in the form of highly-balanced cattlefeed, animal health care, facilities for artifical insemination, and high milk-yielding cross-bred cows.

In almost all of the villages of the Kaira district, cooperative societies managed on democratic lines sprung up and the exposure of the farmers to the organization and technology of modern dairying stimulated a wide range of changes in other areas of their social and economic life.[4] The changed outlook along with a substantial supplementary income, which small landowners in villages began to receive, were very effective contributions to rural development.

As AMUL grew in stature and recognition as an organization which had effectively helped the milk producers, most of whom were marginal farmers, the bargaining hand of the technocrats within the organization vis-a-vis the politicians was strengthened still further. By 1962, and when AMUL had emerged as an effective organization which had done so much for the district, the politicians were inclined to agree to most of the things which the technocrats wanted.

Still the politicians could not be totally written off, not in democratic India, where there are lasting reminders of the longest nationalist freedom movement in recent history. They survived in their secondary position, and at times did not fail to assert themselves effectively.

Admittedly, AMUL dairy, in its formative years, owed its goal, perspective, and direction to the politicians. They organized and led the struggle of the milk producers against the unjust monopoly regulations foisted on them during the alien rule. While Sardar and Desai spoke vaguely of a cooperative organization for the milk producers, TK, ND, Bhagwandas, etc., all of whom had come through the struggles of the Indian national movement, thought through the problem of actually building the organization from a basic village unit spread over nearly one thousand villages. And despite a number of squabbles amongst themselves, they went into the villages and mobilized public support for the new organization.

But that is as far as they could go. The problems of an industrial plant with pasteurization facilities and chilling centres, engineering equipment for manufacturing milk products, milk collection and milk testing for its fat content, payment of cash twice a day, transportation, veterinary services, artificial insemination, balanced cattlefeed, and above all packing and marketing were all beyond them.

Once a village was inducted into the cooperative network, the responsibility of the politician shifted to concern for the communication of grievances, the treatment of labor problems, the effect on the municipality, and occasionally the attitudes of his fellow politicians, of the party organization and of the government. It was for help with these highly specialized political problems, for which the technocrats had neither the acumen nor the time nor indeed the patience, that AMUL often turned to the politicians. By and large the technocrats looked at the politicians as a necessary evil. Naively, and frivolously, some of them even spoke of the virtue of a firmer rule possibly under an illiberal political regime when they wouldn't have to deal with the meddlesome and corrupt politicians. In their desire to improve matters they found that the democratic process with its numerous failings slowed down the undertaking of highly urgent measures. But since the process was there, they adjusted their own style of action to it.

So far as the decision-making within the apex body, namely, the board of directors, was concerned, the managing director and his top associates were the only technical people around. And still the deliberations within the board reflected a near total confidence in the work of the technocrats. The board often gave a free hand to the technocrats knowing full well that most of the decisions they made were of a technical nature and therefore best left to them.

Sometimes new members of the board, who either came through the electoral process or were nominees of government, complained of the lack of participation and consultation. But these complaints were often brushed aside by TK and his successors who depended so heavily on the technocrats to run the organization. In the final analysis what carried the day was the continuing success of the organization right from its inception. As long as it was there, the politicians could not justifiably interfere; they merely tentatively tried.

Within the apex body, the politicians themselves, as might be expected, were not without cleavages of their own. Such cleavages were based on a clash of personalities, party affiliation, or genuine differences in perspective. At such moments the technocrats were often required to play the role of arbiter. They would then indicate in broad terms the kind of policy needed, carefully avoiding the partisan political minefield and sticking to issues which would serve the public interest the best. In other words, the technocrats not only prevailed in the internal working of the organization but also became the definers of the public good. In so doing they often entered into an arena of general well-being which was the traditional preserve of the politicians. Vis-a-vis the technocrats the politicians were often in a no-win situation. They frequently had to depend on the technocrats to bail them out of paralysing political disputes. The more they argued and differed with their fellow-politicians, the more they had to surrender the ultimate decision-making and formulation of policy to the technocrats.

In matters relating to the expansion of organization, the technocrats, with their technical presentation of feasibility studies, blueprints, charts, computer printouts, etc., made points which were much above the head of the average politician. Very few of these politicians had the necessary time to study the case in advance or the ability to extract a set of rival inferences from the same data or even question the underlying assumptions of the points made.

At the same time the operation of a vast organization such as AMUL, which in 1982 received and processed as much as one million litres of milk per day, and its own pace of development, created problems of a political nature which were clearly beyond the capacity of technocrats to solve. AMUL faced the perennial problem of demand for higher wages, improved conditions of work, facilities, etc., from its unionized labor. It also faced demands from secretaries of nearly one thousand village level milk cooperatives for greater participation in decision-making. In addition, there were the problems relating to the municipal, commercial and industrial elite of Anand who found AMUL indifferent to the concerns and sensitivities of the people of the town. For the resolution of these, and many other problems the technocrats had to depend on the politicians.

Given the nature of the dairy industry, both in terms of the perishability of milk and the village-based milk producer, the interdependence of the technocrats and politicians cannot be overemphasized. The perishability of milk, unlike sugar, edible oil, cotton, etc., required the organization to work efficiently and in accordance with the clock. Only the technocrats, given a free hand, could provide this efficiency.

Nonetheless, in mobilizing support for the cooperative organization at the grassroots level, at least in the earlier years, the importance of the politicians could not be overlooked. In the 1950s and 1960s the contribution of the politicians in this respect was indispensable. However, once the organization got itself established, the new villages did not require persuasion by politicians. This work was undertaken by veterinarians and their associates. They set up committees in various villages, by means of elections, and explained how the village-level organization would work. The finer points were picked up by the villagers themselves when the scheme became operational.

The importance of the politicians, however, did not end when organization was complete. They continued to keep an eye on the political process, which often brought into prominence different rural leaders in the far-flung district organization who could then be won over to their side by means of a promise of political support. The politicians also dealt with the municipality, the trade union, the party, and the government leaders by means of the long-cultivated political skill of give-and-take and mutual accommodation.

All in all, the more the technocrats and politicians worked as a team with an acknowledged sense of interdependence, mutually-respected jurisdiction, and above all accommodation, the smoother was the functioning of the cooperative organization.

(iii) *Political Stresses and Strains*

While the politicians *within* the organization learned to function with the technocrats—after the customary several exploratory rounds of meddle-someness and rebuffs—with a sense of separate jurisdiction, mutual respect, accommodation, and tolerance, those *outside* it looked on the dairy organization as one of the many public institutions of society to be controlled and used as a means of enhancing one's own political advantage. In a sense the temptation to do so was understandable. Since the district elected two members to the *Lok Sabha* (Parliament) and eight members to the *Vidhan Sabha* (Legislative Assembly in the state), the control of the organization, the outsiders believed, would also help them to control the district politically. To prevent such an abuse, TK, the politician, and Kurien, the technocrat, had established a healthy political tradition of not using the organization of milk cooperatives for partisan purposes. Such a tradition—an apolitical tradition—, spread to the other cooperatives in Gujarat as well as elsewhere in India. Unfortunately, the case of the sugar cooperatives in the neighbouring state of Maharastra was materially different. There, the cooperative was actively used by politicians for partisan purposes.

The AMUL dairy was identified with the Congress from the very start. It owed its existence to two strong impulses one economic, the other nationalist. It sought to give a fair economic deal to the farmers who were being exploited by Polson and the other milk traders. As well it became a symbol of opposition to the fiat of an alien rule which imposed monopoly restrictions on milk producers to suit its own convenience. The subsequent association of AMUL with Sardar Patel, Morarji Desai, and TK, all staunch Congressmen of that time, made the organization a target of criticism for the non-Congress party organizations. But each time, during and after elections, good sense prevailed and AMUL was spared any deep involvement in partisan strife. No matter what the partisan criticism, it was effectively dealt with by people at all levels of the organization.

To begin with, the farmers at the grassroots level were unreceptive to the criticism of AMUL by campaigning politicians. Since the villagers did not welcome such criticism, the majority of the leaders themselves warned campaigning politicians not to bring AMUL into partisan controversies. Sometimes the villagers themselves warned non-Congress leaders not to make an issue of AMUL since they depended on it for their livelihood.

TK, the Congressman of that time, carefully warned his partymen against the temptation to use the AMUL organization for partisan purposes. In 1962, for instance, the Congress party had fared very badly in the election in the district of Kaira. It was, therefore, feared that in 1967 TK and his partymen would use the organization to improve their electoral fortunes. TK, however, scrupulously kept the organization out of his electoral activity and his party colleagues followed his example.

The technical staff of AMUL, especially the senior members, who had come from different parts of India, had no partisan interest and were most keen to keep their organization out of party politics. They, therefore, carefully watched and monitored moves made by their subordinates in the district.

Above all, TK and the AMUL board of directors established the tradition of paying their political adversaries high respect and sometimes they even elected them to and associated them with various committees. Such a gesture often helped them to earn the good will of their erstwhile adversary once the electoral rhetoric and strife died down. This, in turn, helped the organization to avoid partisanship in its decision-making.

AMUL's major problems came with the appearance of the Janata party and the domination of the Congress by Indira Gandhi. This Congress in its relations with all major public institutions proved to be intolerant and unaccommodating. Accordingly after 1980, AMUL, had its first taste of uncompromising politicians. Nevertheless, because of its long-standing tradition of give-and-take it was able to tone down the fierceness of partisan politics introduced by men who belonged to this new Congress (1).

The politicians at the level of the state refrained, as a rule, from interfering with the working of AMUL. The interference from New Delhi, particularly in the affairs of the National Dairy Development Board (NDDB), which grew out of the experiences of AMUL, was another matter. To that we now turn.

In 1964, Lalbahadur Shastri, the then Prime Minister of India, went to Anand to inaugurate a cattlefeed factory. During the occasion, Shastri also addressed a large group of farmers. What Shastri saw in Anand he could scarcely believe. The farmers there, since the establishment of AMUL, had made great advances. Shastri turned around to its architect, namely Kurien, and asked him to build a cooperative dairly like AMUL in every district of India.

In 1965, NDDB was established in Anand to fulfil Shastri's wishes to replicate AMUL in the different districts of India. The AMUL-type cooperative was dubbed "the Anand pattern" and Kurien and his fellow-technocrats started to work on the problems of an organizational and technical nature necessary before such a colossal undertaking could be launched. These problems were, relatively speaking, not as difficult as the problems posed by the vested interests, the bureaucracy, headstrong and corrupt politicians, and above all, the unavailability of dedicated rural leaders and social workers. Not all parts of India were equally politically mobilized during the Indian freedom movement. Such a movement had given rise to its own rural leadership and had also brought into action many dedicated social workers. These together had proved to be a very valuable resource in launching milk cooperatives and other social activities which depended on large-scale public involvement. For its part, the NDDB came out with an ambitious programme known as Operation Flood I (and later Flood II) and hoped that this would stimulate a commensurate rural leadership able to organize and operate the newly-established milk cooperatives.

Towards the implementation of such a programme, the FAO, under its World Food Programme, provided to the NDDB an initial investment of $100m. (Later through Operation Flood II, and other related schemes, Kurien and his associates were able to get aid, etc. to a total of nearly one billion dollars.)

Such vast funds added to the fact that organizational extension and control were in the hands of the NDDB made it a target of politicians' greed, bureaucrats' hunger for power, and journalists' and academics' ability to destroy or enhance the positive image of the undertaking. Almost every agriculture minister in New Delhi either wanted the NDDB to establish a milk cooperative in his constituency or to give him funds to invest where he thought they would help the agricultural economy of his district and at the same time enhance his own political hold on the area. A number of bureaucrats in the agricultural ministry who could not always withstand the presence of a vast, effective, and result-producing organization like the NDDB created obstacles by means of government regulations of all kinds. However, what saved the day for the technocrats of the NDDB was the Prime Minister's office, either under the Congress, Janata, or Congress (I). Since AMUL and NDDB, with their substantial achievements, became literally the show pieces of the nation, especially when visiting dignitaries were brought in to be shown the extent of India's dairy development, the Prime Minister's office repeatedly told the ministers and bureaucrats to stop their interference. Despite this, some interference did continue in the form of delays in permission for expansion and snide remarks in official correspondence.

Barring a few notable exceptions, the journalists and academics warmly endorsed the achievements of the technocrats of NDDB, often, however, qualifying their endorsements by saying that they had "a long way to go" before their efforts could be described as successful.

While the technocrats of NDDB fought their way through the obstacles of vested interests, self-seeking politicians, and needless bureaucratic regulations in the various states of India where they launched their programmes, the nature of their success in reality depended upon the quality of response which they received from the average milk producer and the grassroots organizations in the various villages. Such a response, where intensive research still remains to be done, is bound to be mixed for the simple reason that these technocrats are operating in a vast and varied country. Nevertheless, what they have missed in other states is the kind of response which TK and his associates provided in the district of Kaira, and as a result of such a precedent, in other districts of Gujarat.

In terms of their own operation, the technocrats of NDDB have armed themselves, by means of various policy regulations, in such a way that the interference of the politicians and bureaucrats in the affairs of a newly-established cooperative organization can be minimized. In actual practice, however, such a defence mechanism does not provide for protection against all operational actualities. The NDDB, an outgrowth of AMUL, working in a different social and political terrain, thus provides an example of the difficulty of having to work in situations where relationships between the technocrats and politicians are unpredictable. It is just this unpredictability that makes relationships materially different from AMUL's, where jurisdictional sense, the spirit of give-and-take, and above all, the excitement of working for something vastly greater than personal gain, have together made the relationship between the technocrats and politicians exemplary.

NOTES

1   This paper is based on repeated interviews of technocrats, veterinarians, politicians, and milk producers in various districts of Gujarat. The interviews were spread over fifteen years, from 1967 to 1982. Sometimes the same respondents were interviewed again and again over an extended period of time.
2   See in this connection A. H. Somjee, "Social Mobility and Tensions Among the Patidars of Kaira" in *Contributions to Asian Studies*, vol. 12, 1979.
3   See in this connection Chandrakant Shah, *Jillana Dudh Udhyogno Prerak gtiLas* (Anand, Kaira Jilla Dudh Utpadak Sangh Ltd., no date), p. 1.
4   In this connection refer to A. H. Somjee and Geeta Somjee, "Cooperative Dairying and Profiles of Social Change in India", *Economic Development and Cultural Change*, April 1978.

CONTRIBUTORS

JOHN A. AGNEW (Ph.D. Syracuse) is an Associate Professor and Chairman Department of Social Sciences, Maxwell School, Syracuse University. He is the editor of *Innovation Research and Public Policy* (Syracuse, 1980), co-author of *Order and Skepticism: Human Geography and the Dialectic of Science* (Washington, D.C., 1981) and author of articles in *The Professional Geographer, Political Geography Quarterly*, and *Urban Affairs Quarterly* on innovation diffusion and theories of development.

SURINDER M. BHARDWAJ (Ph.D. Minnesota) is Professor of Geography at Kent State University. He is the author of *Hindu Places of Pilgramage in India: A Study in Cultural Geography* (University of California Press, 1973) and he has published articles in several international journals including *Social Science and Medicine, National Geographic Journal of India, Geographical Review, Asian Profile, International Geography* and *Tijdschrift Voor Economische en sociale Geographic.*

CHARLES H. KENNEDY (Ph.D. Duke) is Associate Professor in Department of Government and Legal Studies, Bowdoin College. He was a Senior Fellow of American Institute of Pakistan Studies (1982) and recently he has been awarded Fullbright Fellowship and travel grant to conduct research in Pakistan. Professor Kennedy has contributed articles to several scholarly journals including *Journal of Commonwealth* and *Comparative Politics, Journal of South Asian and Middle Eastern Studies, Pakistan Journal of Public Administration* and has contributed a chapter in Eden Nabi (ed.) *Muslim Ethnic Minorities in the Middle East* (Syracuse, 1982).

YOGENDRA K. MALIK (Ph.D. Florida) is a Professor of Political Science at the University of Akron, Ohio. He is the author of several books including *East Indians in Trinidad: A Study in Minority Politics* (Oxford, 1971), *North Indian Intellectuals: An Attitudinal Profile* (Brill, 1979) and editor of *Politics and the Novel in India* (Orient Longman, 1979) and, *South Asian Intellectuals and Social Change* (Heritage, 1982). He has contributed articles to several international journals including *Journal of Politics, Western Political Quarterly, Asian Survey, Comparative Educationa Review, Asia Quarterly, Political Science Review, Indian Journal of Public Administration* and others.

DHIRENDRA K. VAJPEYI (Ph.D. Michigan State) is a Professor of Political Science at the University of Northern Iowa. He is the author of *Modernization and Social Change in India* (Manohar, 1979) and is a co-author of *Government and Politicis in India* (1981). He has contributed articles to several international journals including *Journal of Local Administration Overseas, International Review of History and Political Science, Indian Journal of Political Science, Asian Studies* and *Indian Journal of Public Administration* and others.

LAKSHMAN YAPA (Ph.D. Syracuse) is a Professor of Geography at Pennsylvania State University. He has published articles in many professional journals including *Annals of the Association of American Geographer, The Professional Geographers*, a chapter each in R. S. Ganpathy (ed.) *Agriculture, Rural Energy and Development* (1980), *Proceedings of the International Association for the Advancement of Appropriate Technology for Developing Countries* (Michigan 1981), and John Agnew (ed.) *Innovation Research and Public Policy* (Syracuse, 1980). He is a consultant to USAD & World Bank.

SOMJEE, A. H. (Ph.D. London School of Economics) is a professor of political science at Simon Fraser University, B.C. Canada. Earlier, Professor Somjee taught at Baroda University and University of Durham. He also taught at Oxford University and currently he is serving as a visiting professor at Harvard. Professor Somjee is author of several books including *Political Philosophy of John Dewey, Politics in a Para-urban Community and Democracy and Political Change in Village India: A Case Study*. He has published articles in several international journals including *The American Political Science Review, The Journal of Politics, Political Studies, Contributions to Asian Studies*, and *Asian Survey.*

Journal of Asian and African Studies, XVII, 1-2 (1982)

INDEX